Öffentliche Wirtschaft

Public Enterprise: the Public Sector of the Economy

Handbuch der
Internationalen
Rechts-
und Verwaltungssprache

Manual of
International Legal and
Administrative
Terminology

Herausgeber
Internationales Institut
für Rechts- und
Verwaltungssprache

Editor
International Institute
for Legal and
Administrative Terminology

Deutsch/Englisch

German/English

Carl Heymanns Verlag KG · Köln · Berlin · Bonn · München

Öffentliche Wirtschaft

Public Enterprise: the Public Sector of the Economy

Deutsch/Englisch

German/English

Carl Heymanns Verlag KG · Köln · Berlin · Bonn · München

Dieser Band wurde von der nachstehenden Kommission des Internationalen Instituts für Rechts- und Verwaltungssprache erarbeitet:

Vorsitzender: Karl Kühne	Dr.rer.pol., Hauptverwaltungsrat, Kommission der Europäischen Gemeinschaften, Brüssel
Norman Perry	B.A., Ph.D., FBIM, Head of Central Unit, Inner Cities Initiative, Department of Employment, London
Robert Shaw	B.Phil., M.A., Senior Lecturer, Department of Political Economy, Aberdeen University, Aberdeen
Schlußredaktion:	Ständiges Sekretariat Internationales Institut für Rechts- und Verwaltungssprache Postanschrift: Fehrbelliner Platz 2 D-1000 Berlin 31 Tel.: (030) 867 4162/4165

Abgeschlossen im September 1985

CIP-Kurztitelaufnahme der Deutschen Bibliothek

Handbuch der internationalen Rechts- und Verwaltungssprache /Hrsg. Internat. Inst. für Rechts- und Verwaltungssprache. – Köln; Berlin; Bonn; München: Heymann.

Teilw. mit Parallelt.: Manual of international legal and administrative terminology. Manuel de terminologie juridique et administrative internationale. Manual de terminologiá internacional juridica y administrativa. Manuale di terminologia internazionale giuridica ed amministrativa. – Auf d. Haupttitels. teilw. auch: International Institute for Legal and Administrative Terminology. Institut International de Terminologie Juridique et Administrative. Instituto Internacional de Terminologia Juridica y Administrativa. Istituto Internazionale per la Terminologia Giuridica ed Amministrativa

NE: Internationales Institut für Rechts- und Verwaltungssprache (Berlin, West); 1. PT; 2. PT; 3. PT; 4. PT
Öffentliche Wirtschaft.
Deutsch/englisch / [erarb.: Karl Kühne ...]. – 1988.
  ISBN 3-452-21018-9
NE: Kühne, Karl [Mitverf.]

© 1988 ISBN 3-452-21018-9
Gedruckt im Druckhaus Bayreuth
Printed in Germany

This volume was compiled by the following commission of the International Institute for Legal and Administrative Terminology:

Chairman: Karl Kühne	Dr.rer.pol., Hauptverwaltungsrat, Kommission der Europäischen Gemeinschaften, Brüssel
Norman Perry	B.A., Ph.D., FBIM, Head of Central Unit, Inner Cities Initiative, Department of Employment, London
Robert Shaw	B.Phil., M.A., Senior Lecturer, Department of Political Economy, Aberdeen University, Aberdeen
Final editing:	Permanent Secretariat International Institute for Legal and Administrative Terminology Postal Adress: Fehrbelliner Platz 2 D-1000 Berlin 31 Tel.: (030) 867 4162/4165

Completed in September 1985

CIP-Kurztitelaufnahme der Deutschen Bibliothek

Handbuch der internationalen Rechts- und Verwaltungssprache /Hrsg. Internat. Inst. für Rechts- und Verwaltungssprache. – Köln; Berlin; Bonn; München: Heymann.

    Teilw. mit Parallelt.: Manual of international legal and administrative terminology. Manuel de terminologie juridique et administrative internationale. Manual de terminologiá internacional juridica y administrativa. Manuale di terminologia internazionale giuridica ed amministrativa. – Auf d. Haupttitels. teilw. auch: International Institute for Legal and Administrative Terminology. Institut International de Terminologie Juridique et Administrative. Instituto Internacional de Terminologia Juridica y Administrativa. Istituto Internazionale per la Terminologia Giuridica ed Amministrativa

    NE: Internationales Institut für Rechts- und Verwaltungssprache (Berlin, West); 1. PT; 2. PT; 3. PT; 4. PT
Öffentliche Wirtschaft.
Deutsch/englisch / [erarb.: Karl Kühne . . .]. – 1988.
    ISBN 3-452-21018-9
NE: Kühne, Karl [Mitverf.]

© 1988 ISBN 3-452-21018-9
Gedruckt im Druckhaus Bayreuth
Printed in Germany

Inhaltsverzeichnis

Seite

Vorbemerkung 8
Quellenhinweis 12
Abkürzungen 14

Einführung

1. Die öffentliche Wirtschaft in der Bundesrepublik Deutschland 16
2. Die öffentliche Wirtschaft in Großbritannien 34
3. Beispiele für Privatisierung 54
4. Organigramm 58
5. Beispiele für öffentliche Unternehmensformen im Vereinigten Königreich   59

Wortgut

6.   Begriffe zur öffentlichen Wirtschaft 60
6.1   Allgemeines (Nr. 1–180) 60
6.2   Begriffe in der Gesetzgebung über Erstellung oder Kontrolle von
       öffentlichen Betrieben (Nr. 181–204) 80
6.3   Kosten, Finanzierung, Besteuerung und Vergabewesen in öffentlichen
       Unternehmen (Nr. 205–445) 86
6.4   Energiewirtschaft (Nr. 446–484) 107
6.5   Sonstige Versorgungswirtschaft, Wasserversorgung, Abwasser-
       entsorgung, Post, Fernmeldewesen (Nr. 485–489) 110
6.6   Verkehrswirtschaft, Schienenverkehr, Luftverkehr, Straßenverkehr,
       Hafenwirtschaft, Wasserstraßen (Nr. 490–511) 112
6.7   Verarbeitende Industrien als öffentliche Unternehmen (Nr. 512–513) ... 113
6.8   Kommunale Unternehmen 114
6.9   Arbeitsrecht und Personalpolitik (Nr. 535–557) 117

Alphabetischer Index Deutsch 121
Alphabetischer Index Englisch 133

Table of contents

Page

Foreword 9
Bibliography 13
Abbreviations 14

Introduction

1.	Public Enterprise in the Federal Republic of Germany	17
2.	Public Enterprise in Great Britain	35
3.	Examples of Privatization	56
4.	Organigram	58
5.	Examples of Forms of Public Enterprises in the United Kingdom	59

Vocabulary

6.	Terms relevant to the Public Sector of the Economy	60
6.1	General terms (No. 1–180)	60
6.2	Terms used in legislation and regulations establishing or controlling public enterprises (No. 181–204)	80
6.3	Costs, finance, taxation and procurement in public enterprises (No. 205–445)	86
6.4	Energy Industries (No. 446–484)	107
6.5	Supply of other Essential Services, Water Supply, Sewage Disposal, Postal Services, Telecommunications (No. 485–489)	110
6.6	Transport Industries, Rail, Air, Road, Ports, Waterways (No. 490–511) ..	112
6.7	Manufacturing Industries Owned As Public Enterprises (No. 512–513) ..	113
6.8	Municipal Enterprises (No. 514–534)	114
6.9	Labour Law and Manpower Issues (No. 535–557)	117

Alphabetical Index German 121
Alphabetical Index English 133

Vorbemerkung

1. Der Gedanke, ein Handbuch der internationalen Rechts- und Verwaltungssprache zu schaffen, ist aus einem praktischen Bedürfnis entstanden. Immer größer wird die Zahl der Fachleute, die in fremder Sprache verhandeln müssen, ausländische Besucher zu betreuen haben oder für internationale Aufgaben im In- und Ausland tätig sind. Dafür ist außer der Allgemeinsprache die Kenntnis der entsprechenden Fachausdrücke und Rechtseinrichtungen des Auslands unerläßlich.
   In den zwei- oder mehrsprachigen Wörterbüchern der Allgemeinsprache und der Fachsprachen erscheint das Wortgut meist alphabetisch. Die Bände des Handbuchs sind dagegen nach Sachgebieten geordnet; neben Übersetzungen bieten sie auch Definitionen, Erläuterungen und sachgebietsgebundene Redewendungen, die in anderen Wörterbüchern nicht in dieser Ausführlichkeit verzeichnet werden können.
   Das Handbuch soll alle Fachgebiete umfassen, auf die sich der internationale Rechts- und Verwaltungsverkehr erstreckt. Es erscheint in Einzelbänden, die eine Auswahl der wichtigsten Begriffe und Benennungen des behandelten Sachgebiets enthalten. Der Benutzer hat daher mit den Bänden des Handbuchs die Möglichkeit, sich über das einschlägige Fachwortgut kurzfristig zu unterrichten.
   Das Internationale Institut für Rechts- und Verwaltungssprache hofft, durch seine Veröffentlichungen die Kenntnis der verschiedenen Rechts- und Verwaltungssysteme zu vertiefen und damit zur besseren Verständigung unter den Völkern beizutragen.

2. Das Wortgut wird einheitlich aufgeführt, und zwar links Deutsch, rechts Englisch.
   a) Begriffe und Benennungen, die in beiden Sprachen inhaltsgleich sind, werden mit = gekennzeichnet.
   b) Begriffe und Benennungen, die in der anderen Sprache mit einem ähnlichen Begriff wiedergegeben werden können, werden mit ± gekennzeichnet.
   c) Begriffe und Benennungen, für die es in der anderen Sprache keine Entsprechungen gibt, werden in der Mitte der betreffenden Spalte mit ≠ gekennzeichnet. Übersetzungsvorschläge und – in Klammern – Erklärungen werden darunter gesetzt.
   d) Begriffe und Benennungen, die sich innerhalb der gleichen Wortstelle wiederholen, werden durch eine Tilde (~) gekennzeichnet.

Foreword

1. The idea of producing a manual of international legal and administrative terms arose from a practical need. The number of specialists who have to conduct negotiations in a foreign language, who have to look after foreign visitors, or who are engaged in international business both in their own country and abroad, is continually increasing. Such persons need to know not only the everyday language of the foreign country, but also the technical terms and the legal institutions of that country.
Bilingual and multilingual dictionaries, whether general or specialized, are normally arranged alphabetically. The volumes of the Manual are, in contrast, arranged according to subject matter. In addition to translations, they will also contain definitions, explanations and technical terms which are not covered in the same detail in other dictionaries.
The Manual is to cover all the specialized fields with which international legal and administrative relations are concerned. It will appear in separate volumes, each one of which will contain the most important concepts and terms in a particular field. The user of the volumes of the Manual will thus be able to acquaint himself quickly with the necessary technical vocabulary.
It is the hope of the International Institute for Legal and Administrative Terminology that its publications will deepen the knowledge of different legal and administrative systems and will thereby contribute to a better understanding between peoples.

2. The vocabulary is uniformly arranged, with German on the left and English on the right.
    a) Concepts and expressions which are synonymous in the two languages are indicated by the sign $=$.
    b) Concepts and expressions which can be translated into the other language by a comparable or similar expression are indicated by the sign $\pm$.

    c) Concepts and expressions for which there are no equivalents in the other language are indicated in the middle of the column by the sign $\neq$. Translations proposed and – in brackets – explanations are placed underneath.

    d) Concepts and expressions which are repeated under the same term are indicated by the sign $\sim$.

3. Die Erklärungen werden auf ein Mindestmaß beschränkt. Sie haben **nicht** die Aufgabe, einzelne Rechtsinstitutionen zu beschreiben, sondern sollen lediglich terminologische Aufklärung geben.

4. Die Ausführungen in diesem Band beziehen sich ausschließlich auf das in der Bundesrepublik Deutschland und dem Vereinigten Königreich Großbritannien und Nordirland geltende Recht, unter besonderer Berücksichtigung des Rechts in Großbritannien, mit Ausnahme der Fälle, die sich ausschließlich auf englisches Recht beschränken.

5. Einzelne Begriffe und Benennungen dieses Bandes werden in anderen Bänden des Handbuchs der Internationalen Rechts- und Verwaltungssprache möglicherweise anders übersetzt. Solche Unterschiede ergeben sich aus der Natur der behandelten Sachgebiete.

3. Explanations have been kept to a minimum. They are **not** intended to describe the individual legal institution, but are merely to provide terminological clarification.

4. This volume has been compiled with reference only to the law valid in the Federal Republic of Germany and in the United Kingdom of Great Britain and Northern Ireland, except where it has been restricted expressly to the law of England.

5. Certain concepts and expressions in this edition might be translated differently in other volumes of the Manual of International Legal and Administrative Terminology. These differences are a result of the material itself in the various specialist fields being examined.

Quellenhinweis

Peter Eichborn und Theo Thiemeyer (Hrsg.) – Finanzierung öffentlicher Unternehmen. Schriften zur öffentlichen Verwaltung und öffentlichen Wirtschaft, Band 50, Baden-Baden 1979

Ernst Forsthoff – Lehrbuch des Verwaltungsrechts, München 1973

Peter Friedrich und Peter Kupsch (Hrsg.) – Die Besteuerung öffentlicher Unternehmen, Schriften zur öffentlichen Verwaltung und öffentlichen Wirtschaft, Band 57, Baden-Baden 1981

Gesellschaft für öffentliche Wirtschaft und Gemeinschaft – Entstaatlichung, Verstaatlichung, Status quo – Europa wohin?, Heft 21 der Schriftenreihe, Baden-Baden 1982

Ludwig Geyer – Entwicklung der Bilanz und Erfolgsrechnung aus der kameralistischen Rechnung, München 1970

Bernd Janson – Rechtsformen öffentlicher Unternehmen in der Europäischen Gemeinschaft, Schriften zur öffentlichen Verwaltung und öffentlichen Wirtschaft, Band 55, Baden-Baden 1980

Hans Peters (Hrsg.) – Handbuch der kommunalen Wissenschaft und Praxis, Dritter Band: Kommunale Finanzen und Kommunale Wirtschaft, Berlin – Göttingen – Heidelberg 1959

Albert Schnettler – Öffentliche Betriebe, Essen 1956

Theo Thiemeyer – Wirtschaftslehre öffentlicher Betriebe, Reinbek bei Hamburg 1975

Friedrich Zeiß – Das Eigenbetriebsrecht der gemeindlichen Betriebe (Loseblattsammlung)

Kontrolle öffentlicher Unternehmen, Schriftenreihe der Gesellschaft für öffentliche Wirtschaft und Gemeinwirtschaft, Band 1, Heft 17, Baden-Baden 1980; Band 2, Heft 20, Baden-Baden 1982

Bibliography

M. Brech – Nationalized Industries, in **The Economic System in the U.K.,** edited by D. Morris, Oxford University Press, 3rd edition 1985.

C. D. Foster – **Politics, Finance and the Role of Economics: An Essay in the Control of Public Enterprise,** Allen and Unwin 1971.

J. Redwood and J. Hatch – **Controlling Public Industries,** Blackwell 1982.

R. Pryke – **The Nationalized Industries: Policies and Performance Since 1968,** Martin Robertson 1981.

The Financial and Economic Obligations of the Nationalized Industries (Cmnd. 1337, 1961).

Nationalized Industries: A Review of Economic and Financial Objectives (Cmnd. 3437, 1967).

The Nationalized Industries (Cmnd. 7131, 1978).

Privatisation of the Water Authorities in England and Wales, HMSO 1986.

Abkürzungen/Abbreviations

AG	Aktiengesellschaft
bzw.	beziehungsweise
Co Ltd	Company Limited
d.h.	das heißt
eg/e.g.	exempli gratia/for example
etc.	et cetera
f.	feminium/weiblich
ff.	folgende
fpl.	femininum pluralis/weiblich Mehrzahl
GB	Great Britain
GG	Grundgesetz
GmbH(s)	Gesellschaft(en) mit beschränkter Haftung
i.d.R.	in der Regel
i.e.	id est/that is
Lkws	Lastkraftwagen
m.	masculinum/männlich
mpl.	masculinum pluralis/männlich Mehrzahl
n.	neutrum/sächlich
NEB	National Enterprise Board
No.	number
npl.	neutrum pluralis/sächlich Mehrzahl
Nr.	Nummer
pl.	pluralis/Plural
PLC	Public Limited Company
s.	siehe
seq.	the following
tp.	translation proposed
u.ä.	und ähnliches
usw.	und so weiter
UK	United Kingdom
VIAG	Vereinigte Industrie-Unternehmungen Aktiengesellschaft
z.B.	zum Beispiel

1. Die öffentliche Wirtschaft in der Bundesrepublik Deutschland

1.1 Vorwort

Die Frage, ob der Staat und die Gemeinden selbst wirtschaften sollen und dürfen, wird unterschiedlich beantwortet, je nachdem ob die herrschende Auffassung stärker von marktwirtschaftlichen oder von dirigistischen Ideen geprägt wird. Der Wirtschaftsform der Bundesrepublik Deutschland, der »Sozialen Marktwirtschaft«, entsprechen ungefähr folgende generelle Grundsätze, die einen Kompromiß darstellen:
- Die erwerbswirtschaftliche Tätigkeit ist grundsätzlich den Privaten vorbehalten;
- eine Eigenwirtschaft der öffentlichen Hand ist anzuerkennen für Wirtschaftstätigkeiten hoheitlicher Art (Tätigkeiten, die zur Erfüllung öffentlicher Aufgaben notwendig sind und hoheitliche Gestaltungsmittel benötigen) sowie für andere Tätigkeiten, die zur Erfüllung öffentlicher Aufgaben unerläßlich sind, aber von Privat nicht erfüllt werden, sei es, daß diese sie nicht erfüllen wollen oder nicht erfüllen können;
- einer besonderen Legitimation bedürfen Wirtschaftsbetätigungen der öffentlichen Hand in Konkurrenz mit privaten Betrieben: hier müssen überwiegende Interessen der Allgemeinheit vorliegen, so die Sicherstellung der Versorgung mit lebensnotwendigen Gütern und Leistungen, die von privater Seite überhaupt nicht oder quantitäts- oder qualitätsmäßig und preislich nicht ausreichend geliefert werden.

Auf der Grundlage dieses Subsidiaritätsprinzips wird die wirtschaftliche Betätigung der Gemeinden durch die Gemeindeordnungen der Länder (in Anlehnung an die §§ 67 ff. der Deutschen Gemeindeordnung aus dem Jahr 1935) beschränkt; für Bund und Länder gibt es Rechtsvorschriften dieser Art in den Haushaltsordnungen nur für die Beteiligung an privatrechtlichen Unternehmen (z.B. § 65 der Bundeshaushaltsordnung). Für zahlreiche Wirtschaftsbetätigungen der öffentlichen Hand gibt es gesetzliche Sonderbestimmungen, so für die Bundesbahn, die Bundespost, die Bundesbank, die Bundesanstalt für Arbeit, die Krankenhäuser, die Sparkassen usw.

Von geringer praktischer Bedeutung ist die Sozialisierungsvorschrift des Artikels 15 des Grundgesetzes geblieben, wonach Grund und Boden, Naturschätze und Produktionsmittel zum Zwecke der Vergesellschaftung durch ein Gesetz, das Art und Ausmaß der Entschädigung regelt, in Gemeineigentum oder in andere Formen der Gemeinwirtschaft überführt werden können.

So wie die öffentliche Wirtschaft einerseits gegenüber der privaten Wirtschaft abzugrenzen ist, so ist andererseits das Feld gegenüber der öffentlichen Verwaltung abzustecken. Zur öffentlichen Verwaltung gehören die Behörden der allgemeinen Hoheitsverwaltung sowie die nichtwirtschaftlichen Institutio-

1. The public sector of the economy in the Federal Republic of Germany

1.1 Foreword

The question whether central and local government ought to, or are allowed to carry on economic activity receives a different answer depending on whether prevailing opinion is more strongly influenced by free market thinking or by dirigiste ideas. The economic form of the Federal Republic of Germany, "the social market economy" corresponds roughly to the following general principles, which represent a compromise:
– industrial and commercial activity is basically reserved for the private sector;

– a public sector of the economy is recognized for economic activities affecting the integrity of the State (activities which are necessary for the fulfilment of public obligations and require State resources for their implementation) and for other activities which are indispensable for the fulfilment of public obligations, but cannot or will not be carried out by the private sector;

– public sector economic activities which compete with private enterprises require particular justification: there has to be an overwhelming public interest, for example in securing the supply of essential goods and services if the private sector could not supply them at all, or in inadequate quantity and quality or at unacceptable prices.

Economic activity by local authorities is limited to this principle of last resort by the local government legislation *(Gemeindeordnungen)* of the *Laender* (based on paragraph 67 et seq. of the German Local Government Regulations 1935); similar legislative requirements are placed on the Federation and the *Laender* by Budget Regulations *(Haushaltsordnungen)* only in respect of participation in enterprises incorporated under private law (eg paragraph 65 Federal Budget Regulations). Many economic activities by public authorities are the subject of special legislative provisions, such as the Federal Railways, Post Office, Central Bank, the Federal Employment Institution, hospitals, savings banks etc.

The power to nationalize found in Article 15 of the Basic Law *(Grundgesetz)*, has been of limited practical significance. Under this provision it is possible to transfer into public ownership or some other form of not-for-profit enterprise land and property, natural resources and means of production, by way of nationalization acts which regulate the nature and extent of compensation.

If, on the one hand, the public sector of the economy is differentiated from the private sector, on the other hand there is a distinction between it and the practice of public administration. The official bodies which carry out the general regulatory functions of the State comprise the public administration, as do

nen der öffentlichen Hand, auch öffentliche Einrichtungen genannt. Letztere dienen als rechtsfähige oder nicht rechtsfähige Anstalten oder Körperschaften des öffentlichen Rechts vornehmlich der Wohlfahrt (z.B. Fürsorgeverbände), kulturellen Zwecken (z.B. Museen) oder der Erziehung (z.B. Kindertagesstätten, Schulen, Universitäten). Die öffentlichen Einrichtungen sind dadurch gekennzeichnet, daß sie nicht mit dem Ziel der Kostendeckung arbeiten und keine betriebliche Organisation aufweisen. Der Bereich der öffentlichen Wirtschaft beginnt demgegenüber bei den Einrichtungen, die eine solche betriebliche Organisation haben (insbesondere ein Rechnungswesen, das die Feststellung des Betriebsergebnisses ermöglicht). Diese öffentlichen Betriebe und öffentlichen Unternehmen arbeiten
- entweder in der Absicht, Gewinne zu erzielen, wobei das erwerbswirtschaftliche Prinzip vielfach durch gemeinwirtschaftliche Aufgabenstellungen der Trägerkörperschaften überlagert wird (z.B. Verkehrs- und Versorgungsunternehmen),
- oder sie streben in Erfüllung ihrer öffentlichen Aufgabe lediglich Kostendeckkung an (z.B. Krankenhäuser, Gebührenanstalten),
- oder sie sind von vornherein angesichts ihrer Aufgabenstellung nur auf die Deckung eines Teiles ihrer Kosten ausgerichtet (z.B. Theater, Stadtbäder).

Soweit öffentliche Betriebe und Unternehmen nur das Ziel der Kostendeckkung (einschließlich der Entwicklungskosten) oder Teilkostendeckung – nicht der Gewinnerzielung – verfolgen, gehören sie zugleich – neben den Genossenschaften und sonstigen nichterwerbswirtschaftlichen Unternehmen z.B. der Gewerkschaften – dem Bereich der »Gemeinwirtschaft« an.

Die öffentliche Wirtschaft in der Bundesrepublik Deutschland tritt in Erscheinung in Form öffentlicher Betriebe und öffentlicher Unternehmen. Die öffentlichen Betriebe sind öffentlich-rechtlich organisiert und haben keine eigene Rechtspersönlichkeit. Die öffentlichen Unternehmen haben dagegen eigene Rechtspersönlichkeit und sind entweder Unternehmen des öffentlichen Rechts oder des Privatrechts. Neuerdings setzt sich im Sprachgebrauch die Tendenz durch, auch die öffentlichen Betriebe als öffentliche Unternehmen zu bezeichnen.

In der Bundesrepublik Deutschland gibt es außerdem privatrechtliche *Holdings* des Staates (z.B. Salzgitter AG, Saarbergwerk AG, Deutsche Industrieanlagen GmbH).

Die Rechtsform genügt indessen nicht, das Verhältnis des Betriebs oder Unternehmens zu seinem Trägerverband ausreichend zu charakterisieren: Rechtliche Selbständigkeit bedeutet nicht immer wirtschaftliche Autonomie und umgekehrt. So ist einerseits wirtschaftliche Autonomie auch ohne rechtliche Selbständigkeit möglich, manchmal sogar in dem Umfang, daß der Träger keinen echten Einfluß mehr hat. Andererseits schützt rechtliche Selbständigkeit in

non-economic institutions in the public domain also known collectively as public facilities *(oeffentliche Einrichtungen)*. The latter are non-departmental public bodies or statutory corporations which may or may not have their own legal personality under public law and primarily serve purposes of social welfare (eg public assistance unions), culture (eg museums) or education and training (eg day nurseries, schools, universities). Public facilities do not have a commercially structured organizational format and do not work towards complete recovery of their costs. In contrast, economic activity in the public sector is characterized by a commercially-structured organization (in particular in its accounting conventions which permit the determination of trading results). Public enterprises and publicly-owned businesses work
– either to make a profit, albeit the wholly commercial principle is often overlain by duties imposed in the public interest by the ultimate owning authority (eg transport and public utility undertakings),

– or they seek at least to cover their costs while discharging their public obligations (eg hospitals, fee-charging institutions in general),
– or their terms of reference from the outset only require that a proportion of operating costs be covered by income (eg theatres, municipal swimming baths).

To the extent that public enterprises and publicly-owned businesses work towards the goal of cost recovery (including developmental costs) or partial cost recovery, rather than profit generation, they also belong to the "not-for-profit" sector *(Gemeinwirtschaft)* together with co-operatives and other non-commercial undertakings eg trade unions.

The public sector of the economy in the Federal Republic of Germany appears in the form of public enterprises and publicly-owned businesses. Public enterprises are organized under public law and have no individual legal personality. Publicly-owned businesses by contrast have legal personality and are businesses incorporated either under public law or private law. In recent times, common speech usage has tended to use the term publicly-owned business *(oeffentliche Unternehmen)* to also describe what are more strictly public enterprises *(oeffentliche Betriebe)*.

There are, in addition, one or two conglomerate holding companies in State ownership (eg *Salzgitter AG, Saarbergwerke AG, Deutsche Industrieanlagen GmbH*).

The legal form and status of an enterprise or business does not suffice completely to define its relationship to the owning organization: legal independence does not always imply business autonomy, and vice versa. Business autonomy is possible without legal independence, sometimes even to the extent that the owning body no longer has any real influence. On the other hand, legal inde-

vielen Fällen nicht vor massiver Einflußnahme des Trägers, vor allem dann, wenn finanzielle Abhängigkeit besteht.

Die Rechtsbeziehungen der öffentlichen Betriebe und Unternehmen zu Dritten (z.b. ihren Benutzern und Kunden) sind grundsätzlich privatrechtlicher Art, in wenigen Ausnahmefällen öffentlich-rechtlicher Natur (z.B. Bundespost).

1.2 Öffentliche Betriebe

Regiebetriebe

Der Regiebetrieb – auch Verwaltungsbetrieb genannt – wird als Teil der Verwaltung der Trägerkörperschaft geführt. Diese Betriebsform war bis zu Beginn dieses Jahrhunderts in Deutschland vorherrschend. Sie ist heute nur noch von geringer Bedeutung, z.B. für Hilfsbetriebe (Verwaltungsdruckereien der Länder, Fuhrpark, Brennstoffversorgung).

Der Regiebetrieb hat weder rechtliche noch wirtschaftliche Selbständigkeit. Der Betriebsleiter ist als Angehöriger des öffentlichen Dienstes an die Anweisungen der übergeordneten Stellen gebunden. Der Regiebetrieb ist in die Haushaltswirtschaft des Gemeinwesens eingegliedert mit der gleichen Etatbindung, wie sie für die sonstigen Bereiche der öffentlichen Verwaltung gilt. Die Einnahmen und Ausgaben werden brutto mit dem erwarteten Überschuß oder Fehlbetrag im Haushaltsplan des Gemeinwesens veranschlagt. Das Rechnungswesen ist bestimmt durch die kameralistische Buchführung. Da diese die Ermittlung von Gewinn oder Verlust durch eine Erfolgsrechnung mangels Abgrenzung des Betriebsvermögens von dem übrigen Vermögen des Gemeinwesens nicht zuläßt, erstellen diese Betriebe über die Kameralbuchführung hinaus zur Messung des betrieblichen Erfolgs sogenannte »Betriebsabrechnungen« mit der Darstellung von Kosten und Erlösen (»Betriebskameralistik«, »gehobene Kameralistik«, die den Begriff eines Betriebsvermögens einführt).

Größere staatliche Regiebetriebe, für die eine Wirtschaftsführung nach Einnahme- und Ausgabeansätzen des Haushaltsplans nicht zweckmäßig ist (z.B. die Bundesdruckerei), genießen haushaltsrechtlich eine gewisse Befreiung von den strengen Regeln der Kameralistik. Bei ihnen gilt das Prinzip der Netto-Etatisierung: Im Haushaltsplan der Trägerkörperschaft wird lediglich der zu deckende Zuschußbedarf oder der ablieferungsfähige Überschuß des Betriebs veranschlagt. Das Betriebsvermögen wird rechnerisch aus dem Vermögen der Trägerkörperschaft ausgegliedert und als Sondervermögen geführt. Das Rechnungswesen ist gekennzeichnet durch die kaufmännische doppelte Buchführung. Abgesehen von diesen Besonderheiten des Rechnungswesens unterliegen jedoch die Betriebsleitungen der genannten Regiebetriebe bei ihrer Geschäftsführung voll den Weisungen der vorgesetzten Dienststelle, als deren Beauftragte sie im Namen der Trägerkörperschaft im Rechtsverkehr handeln.

pendence is in many cases no protection against the exercise of massive influence by the owning body, in particular when financial dependency exists.

The legal relationships between public enterprises and publicly-owned bodies and third parties (eg their consumers and clients) are basically structured under private law, although in a few cases (eg the Post Office) public law is the regulator.

1.2 Public Enterprises

Trading Funds *(Regiebetriebe)*

A trading fund enterprise, or administrative enterprise, is run as part of the administration of its parent body. This model was dominant in Germany up to the beginning of the century but is now of only minor importance, eg for ancillary service activities (official printers of the *Laender* governments, transport pool, fuel supply).

A trading fund enterprise in Germany (the term 'trading fund' in English administrative usage partially covers both the German terms '*Regiebetrieb*' and '*Eigenbetrieb*') has neither legal nor economic independence. Its chief executive is a public servant who is bound by instructions from higher levels of the administration. The trading fund is incorporated into the general fiscal arrangements of public administration and subject to the same budgetary regulations. Its revenue and outgoings are included in the budget estimates of its parent body without netting off the anticipated surplus or deficit. Book-keeping is done within the framework of public service accounting conventions *(Kameralistik)*. This method does not allow the identification of profit or loss through an analysis of trading results because it is not legally possible to separate the assets of the enterprise from the rest of the assets of the public body. It is thus normal practice for trading funds to prepare trading accounts *(Betriebsabrechnungen)* to measure commercial performance, which include costs and income *(Betriebskameralistik)* and which also include capital items with provision for depreciation *(gehobene Kameralistik)*.

The larger State trading funds, which cannot realistically be managed on the basis of income and expenditure estimates in administrative accounts (eg the Federal Printing Office), benefit from amended budget regulations which free them to a certain extent from the rigid rules of the single-entry public service conventions. They are allowed to conduct budgeting on a net basis *(Nettoetatisierung)*. The budget estimates of the parent body include only an item for any surplus delivered by the enterprise or a deficit which has to be covered. The assets of the enterprise are, for accounting purposes, separated from the main assets of the owning body and treated as a special fund. Commercial double-entry accounting conventions are used. However, apart from these distinctive accounting features, the managers of these enterprises are wholly subordinate on a day-to-day basis to the higher levels of the administration and, in any legal matters, act as their representatives in the name of the owning body.

Eigenbetriebe

Weiter geht die wirtschaftliche Verselbständigung bei den Eigenbetrieben der Gemeinden. Diese Organisationsform – im Jahr 1938 durch die Eigenbetriebsverordnung geschaffen und inzwischen in den Bundesländern landesgesetzlich geregelt – sollte vor allem der völligen Verselbständigung kommunaler Betriebe durch Gründung von privatrechtlichen Gesellschaften entgegenwirken. Der Eigenbetrieb hat sich bewährt und dient insbesondere vielen kommunalen Verkehrs- und Versorgungsunternehmen als Betriebsform; auch einige Länder haben Eigenbetriebe.

Der Eigenbetrieb ist – außer durch seine rechnungsmäßige Ausgliederung aus der Kommunalverwaltung – durch eine Verselbständigung des Managements gekennzeichnet, die eine freiere Wirtschaftsführung gestattet. Der Gemeinderat hat als unmittelbar übergeordnete Instanz des Eigenbetriebs über wichtige Fragen der Unternehmensführung (z.B. die Feststellung des Wirtschaftsplans und des Jahresabschlusses, die Darlehensaufnahme und die Tarifgestaltung) zu beschließen. Demgegenüber ist die Werkleitung für die laufende Betriebsführung allein verantwortlich. Ein aus Gemeindevertretern und zuweilen auch aus Arbeitnehmervertretern bestehender Werkausschuß (Verwaltungsrat) nimmt an der Unternehmensführung teil und übt die ständige Aufsicht über die Werkleitung aus.

Der Eigenbetrieb wird im übrigen finanzwirtschaftlich als Sondervermögen verwaltet. Auf der Grundlage kaufmännischer doppelter Buchführung wird in einem Jahresabschluß, bestehend aus der Jahresbilanz und der Jahreserfolgsrechnung, das Betriebsergebnis ausgewiesen. Grundsätzlich soll der Eigenbetrieb Gewinne erzielen, durch die mindestens eine marktübliche Verzinsung des Eigenkapitals neben angemessenen Rücklagen erwirtschaftet wird. Wo dies nicht möglich ist, sollten die Erträge jedoch mindestens die Aufwendungen decken. Zu den Aufwendungen gehören auch angemessene Abschreibungen, die Steuern und die Zinsen für die zu Zwecken des Betriebs aufgenommenen Schulden. Ein Jahresverlust soll, soweit er nicht aus Haushaltsmitteln der Gemeinde ausgeglichen wird, auf neue Rechnung vorgetragen und aus den Gewinnen der folgenden Geschäftsjahre oder aus dem Rücklagekapital abgedeckt werden.

Erwerbswirtschaftliches Denken zeigt sich auch in der Planung des Eigenbetriebs. Der Eigenbetrieb stellt einen Wirtschaftsplan auf, bestehend aus dem Erfolgsplan, dem Vermögensplan (Finanzplan) und der Stellenübersicht. Der Erfolgsplan tritt an die Stelle des Verwaltungshaushalts der Gemeinde; er enthält alle voraussehbaren Erträge und Aufwendungen des Wirtschaftsjahrs. Der Vermögensplan enthält alle voraussehbaren Einnahmen und Ausgaben des Wirtschaftsjahrs, die sich aus Anlagenänderungen und aus der Kreditwirtschaft des Eigenbetriebs ergeben. Er stellt insbesondere den geplanten Investitionen die

Autonomous Undertakings *(Eigenbetriebe)*

The autonomous undertakings of local authorities take the concept of economic independence a step further. This organizational form was created by regulations in 1938 *(Eigenbetriebsverordnung)* and has since been regulated in legislation by the *Laender* of the Federation. Its intention is to provide an alternative for municipal enterprises to the full independence represented by incorporation as companies under private law. The autonomous undertaking has proved itself and provides the operational form in particular for many municipal transport and utility undertakings; a number of *Laender* also have autonomous undertakings.

The *Eigenbetrieb* is characterized not only by its separation in accounting terms from local authority administration, but also by autonomy for its management which permits more flexible operation. The elected members of the local authority, as the direct owners of the undertaking, are responsible for major decisions concerning management direction (eg approving the business plan and the annual accounts, borrowing and price structure). On the other hand, the line management is solely responsible for day-to-day operational matters. A policy setting committee comprising local authority representatives and, in some cases, representatives of the workforce takes a part in directing the enterprise and exercises routine supervision over line management.

In financial terms, an *Eigenbetrieb* is treated as a special fund *(Sondervermögen)*. Using commercial double-entry book keeping, trading results are presented in annual accounts which consist of the annual balance sheet and a financial statement for the year. An *Eigenbetrieb* is basically charged with achieving sufficient profits to permit market-oriented depreciation of its owner's equity plus reasonable provision to reserves. Where this is not possible, receipts should at least cover outgoings. These are usually defined to include certain writing-down of assets, taxation and interest on debt taken on for operational reasons. Any loss, to the extent that it is not made good from the resources of the local authority, is carried forward and covered either from profits in the following financial year, or from the reserve fund.

A commercial approach is also visible in the planning of an autonomous undertaking *(Eigenbetrieb),* whose corporate plan consists of a profit and loss forecast, a resources (finance) plan, and a manpower forecast. The profit and loss forecast substitutes for the administrative budget of the local authority; it contains all the anticipated revenues and outgoings in the financial year. The resources plan contains all the items of income and costs in the financial year which arise from changes in the asset structure and the financing of borrowing. In particular it sets out the cover for planned investment, whether by depreci-

Deckungsmittel aus Abschreibungen, Rücklageentnahmen, Kapitalzuführungen der Gemeinde sowie Anleiheerlösen, die aus dem Vermögenshaushalt der Gemeinde zugeleitet werden, gegenüber.

Trotz der Verselbständigung von Geschäftsführung und Rechnungswesen besitzt der Eigenbetrieb keine eigene Rechtsfähigkeit. Die Geschäftsleitung – in der Regel nicht Beamte, sondern Angestellte – handelt nicht für den Eigenbetrieb als solchen, sondern für die Gemeinde, die Träger von Rechten und Verbindlichkeiten aus der Geschäftsführung des Eigenbetriebs ist.

Eine Sonderstellung in den Organisationsformen haben die Bundesbahn und die Bundespost. Sie sind wie die Eigenbetriebe autonome Wirtschaftskörper (Sondervermögen) ohne volle eigene Rechtspersönlichkeit, darüber hinaus aber Dritten gegenüber rechts- und parteifähig. Sie können im Rechtsverkehr unter ihrem Namen handeln, klagen und verklagt werden. Auch bestehen – anders als bei den Eigenbetrieben – Haftungsbeschränkungen; rechtlich (nicht tatsächlich) haftet der Bund nicht für die Verbindlichkeiten dieser Sondervermögen.

1.3 Öffentlich-rechtliche Unternehmen

Im Gegensatz zu den Betriebsformen der Regiebetriebe und Eigenbetriebe scheiden die öffentlich-rechtlichen Unternehmen vollständig aus dem Gemeinwesen aus: Sie treten als selbständige juristische Personen des öffentlichen Rechts mit eigenem Vermögen und Rechnungswesen (Wirtschaftsplan, Jahresabschluß) sowie eigener Wirtschaftsführung neben das Gemeinwesen. Sie handeln im eigenen Namen durch ihre Organe (Vorstand, Verwaltungsrat). Da es ein allgemeines Statut des öffentlich-rechtlichen Unternehmens – vergleichbar den zwingenden Normen des Gesellschaftsrechts für das privatrechtliche Unternehmen – bislang nicht gibt, kann die Organisation des öffentlich-rechtlichen Unternehmens von Fall zu Fall den jeweiligen Zielsetzungen angepaßt werden. Dies geschieht z.B. bei der Festsetzung von Haftungsbeschränkungen für den Trägerverband oder bei der Regelung der Beziehungen des Unternehmens zu seinen Benutzern, die privatrechtlicher, zuweilen aber auch öffentlich-rechtlicher Natur sein können.

Diese Unternehmen können in der Rechtsform der Körperschaft des öffentlichen Rechts oder der rechtsfähigen Anstalt des öffentlichen Rechts geführt werden. Zum Wesen der öffentlichen Körperschaft gehört die Selbstverwaltung durch ihre Mitglieder bei grundsätzlicher Beschränkung des Einflusses der öffentlichen Hand auf die Rechtsaufsicht. Demgegenüber ist die Anstalt eine Personen- und Sachgesamtheit, die in der Hand eines Trägers öffentlicher Verwaltung einem öffentlichen Zweck dient. Die Einflußnahme der öffentlichen Hand geht bei ihr weiter als bei der öffentlich-rechtlichen Körperschaft.

ation, provision from reserves, capital injection from the local authority, or the proceeds of bonds issued by the authority from its own resources budget.

Despite its autonomy in operational and accounting matters, an autonomous undertaking *(Eigenbetrieb)* is not a separate legal entity. Operational management is usually run by employees rather than permanent public officials (an important distinction in Germany) but they act not on behalf of the undertaking as such, but in the name of the local authority, which carries all the rights and obligations arising from the operation of the undertaking.

The Federal Railways *(Bundesbahn)* and Federal Post Office *(Bundespost)* have a special position in terms of organizational form. Like autonomous undertakings *(Eigenbetriebe)* they are an autonomous economic entity (special fund) without distinctive legal personality, but they can take legal action and make legal agreements against and with third parties. They can take part, in their own name, in any legal activity, negotiate, sue and be sued. Unlike other autonomous undertakings, there are limitations on their liability in law; in strict legal terms (though not in reality) the Federal Government does not guarantee the obligations of these special funds.

1.3 Enterprises Incorporated under Public Law

In contrast to the organizational format of the trading fund *(Regiebetrieb)* and the autonomous undertaking *(Eigenbetrieb)*, enterprises incorporated under public law step completely out of the sphere of public administration. They stand parallel to public administration, as self-contained legal personalities under public law, with their own resources and accounting procedures (corporate plan, annual accounts) and their own management structure. They do business in their own name through their own decision-making bodies (executive board, supervisory board). Since there is still no general legislation governing public-law enterprises comparable to the strict norms of company law for enterprises incorporated under private law, the organization of public-law enterprises can be adapted to whatever are the policy objectives in particular cases. This can happen, for example in determining the limitations on liability for the ultimate owning body, or in setting the relationship between an enterprise and its users which can be made to conform to private law or public law conventions as required.

These kinds of enterprise can be run in the legal form of a public corporation *(Körperschaft des öffentlichen Rechts)* or as a non-departmental public body *(Anstalt des öffentlichen Rechts)* with its own legal status. The essence of a public corporation is independent administration by its board members with the influence of public authorities limited basically to legal supervision. In contrast, an *Anstalt* is a combination of staff and resources set up by the public administration to serve a public objective. The extent of influence by public authorities is considerably greater than with a public corporation.

Die Körperschaft des öffentlichen Rechts findet sich nur vereinzelt als Organisationsform der öffentlichen Wirtschaft; wichtigstes Beispiel sind die Sozialversicherungsträger. Rechtsfähige Anstalten des öffentlichen Rechts sind z.b. die Rundfunkanstalten, die öffentlich-rechtlichen Versicherungsinstitute der Privatversicherung sowie die Kreditinstitute des Bundes (Bundesbank, Kreditanstalt für Wiederaufbau), der Länder (Landesbanken) und der Gemeinden (Sparkassen).

Öffentlich-rechtliche Unternehmen sind auch die Zweckverbände. Dies sind überörtliche Zusammenschlüsse von Gemeinden zur gemeinsamen Unterhaltung eines Betriebs, die das Eigenbetriebsrecht nicht ermöglicht. Wegen der geringen wirtschaftlichen Beweglichkeit des Zweckverbandes wird jedoch in solchen Fällen vielfach auf die Gestaltungsformen des Privatrechts zurückgegriffen (z.B. AG, GmbH).

1.4 Privatrechtliche Unternehmen

Gemischtwirtschaftliche Unternehmen

Das gemischtwirtschaftliche Unternehmen ist eine private Kapitalgesellschaft (Aktiengesellschaft, Gesellschaft mit beschränkter Haftung), an der neben privatem Kapital die öffentliche Hand beteiligt ist. Solche Unternehmen gehören zum Bereich der öffentlichen Wirtschaft, wenn die öffentliche Hand rechtlich oder tatsächlich einen beherrschenden Einfluß auf das Unternehmen ausüben kann (z.B. bei Beteiligung mit mehr als 25%, Mehrstimmrechtsaktien usw.). Bekannte Beispiele sind das Rheinisch-Westfälische Elektrizitätswerk sowie das Volkswagenwerk.

Das gemischtwirtschaftliche Unternehmen untersteht bezüglich seiner Organisation und seiner Geschäftsführung dem Privatrecht (Handels- und Gesellschaftsrecht). Da hier private Interessen gleichberechtigt neben die gemeinwirtschaftlichen Zielsetzungen des öffentlichen Gemeinwesens treten, kann es zu Interessenkollisionen kommen, deren Lösung von dem Verhältnis der Kapitalanteile beider Gruppen, der jeweiligen Zusammensetzung der Organe und der Wirksamkeit von Nebenabreden abhängt. Das Haushaltsrecht verpflichtet die Vertreter der öffentlichen Hand – vor allem, wenn diese sich in der Kapitalminderheit befindet – sich durch geeignete Abmachungen den nötigen Einfluß auf die Geschäftsführung der Gesellschaft, insbesondere eine angemessene Vertretung im Aufsichtsrat, zu sichern. Die Gründung solcher Unternehmen erfolgt häufig aus dem Zwang heraus, große Projekte durch private und durch öffentliche Kapitalgeber gemeinsam zu finanzieren.

Die Rechtsform des gemischtwirtschaftlichen Unternehmens ist in der Praxis überwiegend die der Aktiengesellschaft. Die gemischtwirtschaftlichen Unternehmen gewinnen angesichts der Privatisierungsbemühungen der derzeitigen Koalitionsregierung erheblich an Bedeutung. Schon in den 50er und 60er

Public corporations are found only rarely in the public sector of the economy in Germany; the most important examples are the social security organizations. Examples of legally competent non-departmental public bodies include the broadcasting institutions, those private insurance bodies incorporated under public law, and the financial credit institutions of the Federation (*Bundesbank,* Credit Institute for Reconstruction) the *Laender* (*Land* Banks) and the local authorities (savings banks).

Joint boards *(Zweckverbände)* are also public-law enterprises. They represent the coming together of a number of local authorities to maintain an operational undertaking which cannot be done under the law regulating *Eigenbetriebe*. Because a joint board itself is economically cumbersome, the framework of private law (eg PLC, Co Ltd) is often used as the operating form.

1.4 Enterprises Incorporated under Private Law

Businesses with Mixed Ownership

A mixed ownership business is a private share capital company (PLC, Co Ltd) in which there is a public sector shareholding as well as private capital. These enterprises belong to the public sector of the economy if public authorities can, either in legal terms or in reality, exercise a dominating influence on the firm (eg shareholding in excess of 25%, multivote preference shares etc). Notable examples are the Rhine Westphalia Electricity Utility *(REW – Rheinisch – Westfaelisches Elektrizitaetswerk),* and the *Volkswagen* car firm *(Volkswagenwerk)*.

A mixed ownership business runs its organization and operation under private law (commercial and company law). Because private commercial interests have equal validity with public policy objectives, conflicts of interest can and do arise, whose solution depends on the relative capital holdings of the two groups, the current composition of the governing organs and the effectiveness of any subsidiary agreements. Representatives of the public authorities are obliged by budgetary law to seek appropriate agreements with other shareholders through which an influence on the operating policy of the company can be secured, particularly in cases where the public has a minority shareholding. This kind of enterprise is frequently set up because of the necessity for joint private and public sector funding of major projects.

Mixed ownership businesses in practice are overwhelmingly public limited companies. They are gaining substantially in importance in the context of the privatization initiatives being taken by the current coalition Government. As far back as the 1950's and 1960's, governments of similar political composition

Jahren kam es unter Regierungen mit ähnlicher politischer Zusammensetzung zu breitgestreuten Privatisierungsmaßnahmen, mit denen unter anderem Aktien im Nennwert von 81 Millionen DM der Preussag AG, von 525 Millionen DM der Veba AG und von 360 Millionen der Volkswagenwerk AG an »einkommensschwächere« Bevölkerungskreise veräußert wurden; auch einige Aktien der Deutschen Lufthansa AG wurden dabei abgegeben.

In den 70er Jahren kam es unter anderen politischen Vorzeichen zwar auch zu einem gewissen Rückgang der unmittelbaren Bundesbeteiligungen; von 1975 bis 1982 wurden 19 unmittelbare Bundesbeteiligungen verringert oder aufgegeben, wobei es sich allerdings in sieben Fällen lediglich um Beteiligungen von weniger als 20% handelte. Andererseits wuchs in diesem Zeitraum die Zahl der mittelbaren Beteiligungen erheblich an, so daß die Gesamtzahl der mittel- und unmittelbaren Beteiligungen des Bundes und seiner Sondervermögen (Bahn, Post, *ERP* und Ausgleichsfonds) von 697 im Jahre 1970 auf einen Höhepunkt von 985 im Jahre 1979 anstieg. 1980 ging diese Zahl auf 899 zurück, erhöhte sich aber bis 1982 wieder auf 958, um dann abrupt auf 487 Ende 1983 abzufallen.

Letzterer spektakulärer Rückgang war die Folge der formalrechtlichen Unterstellung, daß ab 1983 die 465 Beteiligungen der Veba AG nicht mehr als unmittelbare Bundesbeteiligungen anzusehen seien. Am 26. Oktober 1983 hatte nämlich das Bundeskabinett die Reduzierung der Beteiligung an der Veba AG von 43,75% auf 30% beschlossen, was Anfang 1984 durchgeführt wurde. Diese Beteiligung war bereits durch die Teilprivatisierung 1965 unter 40% gesunken, dann aber unter der sozialliberalen Koalition mit der sogenannten Gelsenberg-Transaktion, die der Schaffung eines nationalen Ölkonzerns dienen sollte, zeitweilig auf 50,1% angestiegen. Dabei hatte man auf die Stimmrechtsbegrenzung für freie Aktionäre verzichtet.

Mit dieser Unterstellung, daß die Veba AG bei einem Anteil der öffentlichen Hand von 30% nicht mehr dem Komplex der öffentlichen Unternehmen zuzurechnen ist, wenngleich noch dem der gemischtwirtschaftlichen Unternehmung, stellt sich die Frage, ob bedeutsame Minderheitsbeteiligungen bei Zersplitterung des übrigen Aktienbesitzes nicht doch noch einen maßgebenden Einfluß der öffentlichen Eigner bedeuten.

Diese Frage war bereits seit längerem im Falle der Volkswagenwerk AG akut, bei der 20% der Aktien dem Bund und weitere 20% dem Land Niedersachsen gehören (seit 1960).

Hier setzt nun der Beschluß des Bundeskabinetts vom 26. März 1985 ein, der im Falle des Volkswagenwerkes einen Abbau dieses Anteils auf 14% durch Nichtteilnahme an Kapitalerhöhungen vorsieht.

Diesem Beschluß und dem darauf vom Finanzministerium veröffentlichten Plan zur Verringerung von Bundesbeteiligungen (BMF-Finanznachrichten 8/85, 27. 3. 1985) kommt insofern grundsätzliche Bedeutung zu, als es sich hier

to today's introduced a variety of privatization measures, for example through the sale of shares – to 'lower-income' groups – in companies such as *Preussag AG* (81 million DM), *Veba AG* (525 million DM), *Volkswagenwerk AG* (360 million DM) and in *Deutsche Lufthansa AG*.

During the 1970's, under different political auspices, there was some reduction of direct Federal participation in enterprises; between 1975 and 1982 direct shareholdings in 19 enterprises were reduced or wholly disposed of although, in 7 cases, shareholdings of less than 20% were involved. On the other hand, the number of direct participations grew substantially so that, between 1970 and 1979, the total of direct or indirect holdings by the Federal Government or its specially designated funds (Railways, Post Office, European Recovery Program, Equalization of War Burdens Fund) rose from 697 to a high point of 985. In 1980 the number fell to 899, then rose again to 985 in 1982 but fell abruptly to 487 at the end of 1983.

This sudden spectacular decline resulted from a legal ruling that 465 holdings of *Veba AG* no longer had to be counted as direct Federal participations. On 26 October 1983, the Federal Cabinet decided to reduce the Government shareholding in *Veba AG* from 43.75% to 30%, and this took place early in 1984. The Government's Veba shareholding had at one time fallen below 40% under a measure of partial privatization in 1965 but had then temporarily risen to 50.1% when the social-liberal coalition made the so-called '*Gelsenberg* transaction' which was intended to help create a national oil company. At that time the Government had waived the restriction of voting rights for private shareholders which would have been the consequence of its absolute majority shareholding.

If it is held that, with a public sector shareholding of 30%, *Veba AG* no longer counts as a public enterprise – albeit it still belongs to the group of businesses with mixed ownership – the question arises as to whether significant minority participations still give the public sector owners decisive influence when the remaining shareholdings are fragmented.

This question has been acute for a long time in the case of *Volkswagenwerk AG* which, since 1960, has had 20% of its shares owned by the Federal Government and a further 20% by the *Land* Government of Lower Saxony.

Of relevance here is the decision by the Federal Cabinet on 26 March 1985 to reduce the Federal shareholding to 14% by not taking up its share of a new capital issue.

This decision and the related publication by the Finance Ministry of a plan to reduce Federal holdings are of fundamental importance to the extent that they introduce a programme of privatization which seeks to convert into mixed-

um ein Privatisierungsprogramm handelt, das folgende bisher rein öffentliche in gemischtwirtschaftliche Unternehmen umwandeln will:
- VIAG AG - bisher (mit Kreditanstalt) 100%, Abbau um 25%,

- Deutsche Pfandbriefanstalt - bisher Bund 67,88%, andere öffentliche Stellen Rest - Abbau auf »einfache Mehrheitsbeteiligung«,
- Deutsche Siedlungs- und Landesrentenbank, bisher 99%, dito.

Privatisierungsmaßnahmen ohne nähere Bezifferung werden dabei angekündigt für folgende Unternehmen (bisher zu 100% in öffentlicher Hand): Industrieverwaltungsgesellschaft mbH (IVG) - Gesellschaft für Nebenbetriebe der Bundesautobahnen mbH - Deutsche Industrieanlagen GmbH - DIAG - und eine Reihe von Beteiligungen der Deutschen Bundesbahn (Schenker & Co., Deutsche Verkehrs-Kreditbank AG, beide bisher 100%).

Bei bisher schon gemischtwirtschaftlichen Beteiligungen der Deutschen Bundesbahn (Deutsches Reisebüro GmbH - DER - bisher 50,1% Bund, 24,08% andere öffentliche Träger - Amtliches Bayerisches Reisebüro - ABR - bisher 55% Bundesbahn) wird ebenfalls eine weitere (Teil-)Reprivatisierung angekündigt.

Bei der Deutschen Lufthansa AG, die in der Liste mit erfaßt war (bisher 74,31% Bund, 1,75% Post, 0,85% Bahn, 3% Kreditanstalt), sind die Pläne auf starken politischen Widerstand gestoßen und dürften nicht zu realisieren sein.

Eigengesellschaften

Eigengesellschaften sind Kapitalgesellschaften, deren gesamtes Kapital einem oder mehreren Gemeinwesen gehört. Diese Rechtsform findet sich insbesondere bei den Banken und Wohnungsbaugesellschaften der Länder, aber auch bei den Verkehrs- und Versorgungsunternehmen der Gemeinden. Da der Vorstand grundsätzlich die Geschäfte in eigener Verantwortung führt, hat die öffentliche Hand keinen unmittelbaren Einfluß im Wege einer Fach- oder Rechtsaufsicht. Sie kann vielmehr nur mittelbar einwirken über ihre Vertreter im Aufsichtsrat, der den Vorstand aus wichtigen Gründen jederzeit abberufen kann.

Die Vorteile der privatrechtlichen Organisationsform liegen für das Gemeinwesen vor allem in der beiderseitigen Haftungsbeschränkung, in der größeren Beweglichkeit der Geschäftsführung sowie der Erleichterung der Kreditbeschaffung. Hinderlich wirken unter Umständen die dem Gläubiger- und Gesellschafterschutz dienenden gesellschaftsrechtlichen Vorschriften, die bei Trägerschaft einer oder mehrerer Gebietskörperschaften ihren Zweck verfehlen. Es kann auch zu Konflikten zwischen den erwerbswirtschaftlichen Zielen des Vorstands und den gemeinwirtschaftlichen Zielen des Trägerverbands kommen, die eine - nicht immer leicht realisierbare - Einschränkung der Befugnisse des Vorstands erforderlich machen.

ownership business a number of enterprises which have until now been wholly in the public sector:
- *VIAG AG* – Previously 100% Federal ownership (with *Kreditanstalt*) – holding to be reduced by 25%,
- *Deutsche Pfandbriefanstalt* – Previously 67.88% Federal ownership, and 32.12% other public bodies – holding to be reduced to 'simple majority',
- *Deutsche Siedlungs- und Landesrentenbank* – Previously 99% ditto.

In addition privatization measures, as yet unquantified, have been announced for a number of enterprises which are wholly in public ownership at the moment: *Industrieverwaltungsgesellschaft mbH (IVG)* – *Gesellschaft für Nebenbetriebe der Bundesautobahnen mbH* – *Deutsche Industrieanlagen GmbH* – *DIAG* – a number of wholly-owned subsidiaries of the Federal Railways, of which the two best known are *Schenker & Co.* and *Deutsche Verkehrs-Kredit-Bank AG*.

Some railway holdings in mixed enterprises have also been announced as targets for further privatization or reprivatization. They include *Deutsche Reisebüro GmbH (DER)* 50.1% Federal participation, 24.08% other public bodies, *Amtliches Bayerisches Reisebüro (ABR)* 55% Federal Railways.

Proposals to privatize *Deutsche Lufthansa AG* (74.31% Federal holding, 1.75% Post Office, 0.85% Federal Railways, 3.00% *Kreditanstalt*) encountered strong political resistance and were not proceeded with.

Wholly-owned Companies

Wholly-owned companies are share-capital companies all of whose shares are owned by one or more public authorities. This particular legal form can be found particularly in the banks and social housing companies belonging to the *Laender,* but also in local authority transport and utility undertakings. Because the executive board has basic responsibility for managing affairs, public authorities have no direct influence via regulatory or legal supervision. Their direct intervention can come only via their representatives on the supervisory board which can at any time, if the circumstances are grave enough, dismiss the executive board.

The advantages of private law organizations to the public sector lie above all in the limitations of liability on both sides, in greater flexibility of operation and the greater ease of raising loan capital. In some circumstances there are hindrances from provisions of company law intended to protect shareholders but which, where the owners are in fact one or more territorial authorities, lose their point. There can also be conflicts between the strictly commercial objectives of the executive board and the public policy interests of the owning bodies which necessitate some limitation on the powers of the executive board which is not always easy to accomplish.

1.5 Öffentlich gebundene Unternehmen
(Betriebsverpachtung, Betriebsführungsvertrag, Konzessionsvertrag)

Es kann sich ergeben, daß das öffentliche Gemeinwesen keine Möglichkeit sieht, einen Betrieb selbst weiterzuführen; vielfach ist aus politischen Gründen indessen eine Erhaltung des Betriebsvermögens für die öffentliche Hand erforderlich, so daß ein Verkauf nicht in Betracht kommt. In solchen Fällen ist die Verpachtung des Betriebsvermögens – im allgemeinen auf längere Zeit – an ein privates Unternehmen zur Wahrnehmung einer öffentlichen Aufgabe ein geeigneter Ausweg.

Eine andere Gestaltungsform ist der Abschluß eines Betriebsführungsvertrags. Das öffentliche Gemeinwesen bleibt in diesem Fall nicht nur Eigentümer, sondern auch Unternehmer. Ein Dritter (z.b. eine Betriebsführungsgesellschaft) führt den Betrieb gegen Entgelt auf Rechnung der Trägerkörperschaft, bei der das Unternehmensrisiko verbleibt.

Der Konzessionsvertrag ist eine häufig anzutreffende Form wirtschaftlicher Betätigung, insbesondere im kommunalen Bereich. Die Gemeinde gestattet mit einem solchen Vertrag Versorgungsunternehmen, Energie oder Wasser in das Gemeindegebiet zu liefern, oder Verkehrsunternehmen, Verkehrsleistungen in diesem Gebiet zu erbringen, und zwar in der Regel unter Ausschließung anderer. Dem Unternehmen wird dabei meistens das ausschließliche Recht eingeräumt, Gemeindeeigentum – vor allem Straßen, Plätze – zur Verlegung von Leitungen oder Schienen zu benutzen. Das Unternehmen zahlt an das Gemeinwesen eine sogenannte Konzessionsabgabe; eine solche wird vielfach auch von Eigenbetrieben – und zwar aus steuerlichen Gründen – abgeführt, wobei die entsprechenden Beträge in der Regel dem Betrieb für Investitionen wieder zur Verfügung gestellt werden.

Die Betriebsverpachtung und der Betriebsführungsvertrag sind privatrechtlicher, der Konzessionsvertrag ist öffentlich-rechtlicher Natur.

1.5 Regulated Enterprises
(Enterprise leasing, management contract, concession contract)

It can happen that a public authority sees no possibility of carrying on an undertaking itself anymore. Political considerations often dictate that the public sector should retain ownership of the assets, so sale does not come into question. In these cases, the assets of the enterprise can be leased to a private company – generally for a long period – so that a way is found of discharging a public task.

Another model is to secure an operations contract. The public not only remains the owner but in this case is also the undertaker. A third party (eg an operating company) runs the enterprise against payment by the owning body, which also remains the carrier of the operating risk.

The concession contract is a commonly encountered form of economic activity particularly in local government. The authority, under this kind of contract, permits utility companies to supply energy or water within its area, or transport undertakings to operate their services, mainly on the basis that other operators are excluded. The enterprise is usually given an exclusive right to use local authority property – mainly roads and open spaces – to lay or divert services and tracks. The enterprise pays the authority a concessionary levy. A similar payment is often required from *Eigenbetriebe* (on taxation grounds), in which case the contribution is usually made available again to the enterprise to facilitate further investment.

Enterprise leasing and management contracts operate under private law, but the concession contract is made under public law.

2. Die öffentliche Wirtschaft in Großbritannien

2.1 Allgemeine Vorbemerkung

In Großbritannien gibt es kein Äquivalent für die Unterscheidung zwischen privatem Recht und öffentlichem Recht, wie sie in Deutschland üblich ist und eine einfache Einordnung von Unternehmen in die private oder öffentliche Wirtschaft ermöglicht. Allerdings gibt es im bürgerlichen Recht die Einteilung in privates Recht und öffentliches Recht, aber diese vollzieht sich auf einer anderen Grundlage: Das öffentliche Recht behandelt die Funktionen des Staates und der öffentlichen Behörden, dieweil das private Recht die Rechte und Pflichten von Einzelpersonen in deren Verhältnis zueinander betrifft. Letzteres umfaßt daher Themen wie das Familienrecht, das Vertragsrecht, Entschädigungen für nach bürgerlichem Recht zu behandelnde Schäden und das Eigentumsrecht bzw. Sachenrecht. Dabei sind die Grenzen zwischen beiden Rechtssphären jedoch nicht klar gezogen, denn für zahlreiche Rechtsbeziehungen gilt, daß der Staat und seine Einrichtungen den normalen Grundsätzen des Privatrechts unterliegen; dies gilt bespielsweise in Vertragsangelegenheiten und bei Vermögensfragen bzw. sachenrechtlichen Fragen.

Die öffentliche Wirtschaft stellt einen Begriff dar, der in Großbritannien selten näher definiert wird. Vielfach wird der Ausdruck mit dem der »nationalisierten Unternehmen« *(nationalized industries)* gleichgesetzt; aber der Bereich der öffentlichen Wirtschaft reicht doch darüber hinaus, denn er umfaßt auch die Tätigkeit der kommunalen Behörden wie beispielsweise die öffentliche Verkehrsversorgung und ferner die Tätigkeit besonderer Instanzen, die von der Zentralverwaltung beispielsweise für regionale Entwicklungsaufgaben gebildet werden. Andererseits ist der Bereich der öffentlichen Wirtschaft sogar enger gezogen als der öffentliche Sektor insgesamt, denn zum letzteren gehören auch die öffentliche Verwaltung, die Streitkräfte und der größere Teil des Erziehungs-, Bildungs- und Gesundheitswesens.

Zwei Charakterzüge sind wesentlich für die öffentliche Wirtschaft, mit denen sie sich unterscheidet von der privaten Wirtschaft einerseits und vom öffentlichen Sektor insgesamt, andererseits. Der erste dieser Wesenszüge ist der, daß die öffentlichen Unternehmen sich im Eigentum des Staates oder der örtlichen Gebietskörperschaften befinden oder doch mindestens diesen gegenüber verantwortlich bleiben. Der zweite Wesenszug ist der, daß die öffentlichen Unternehmen Preise für die Lieferung von Gütern oder Leistungen erheben, und daß diese Preise in großen Zügen den Kosten der Leistungserstellung entsprechen. Diese Kostenentsprechung ist vielfach nur graduell gegeben.

Die Abgrenzung der öffentlichen Wirtschaft läßt sich also nur mit Schwierigkeiten genau vornehmen; es gibt aber auch keine klaren Prinzipien, nach denen festzulegen wäre, warum bestimmte Wirtschaftsbereiche in Großbritannien zur öffentlichen Wirtschaft gehören, während andere als privater Wirtschaftsbe-

2. Public Enterprise in Great Britain

2.1 General

The distinction in Germany between public law and private law, which enables the easy classification of enterprises to either the public sector or the private sector, has no exact counterpart in Great Britain. Civil law in Britain is divided into private law and public law but on a different basis: public law deals with the functions of the State and public authorities, while private law concerns the rights and obligations of individuals among themselves and comprises topics such as family law, the law of contract, compensation for civil wrongs and the law of property. The boundary between the two bodies of law is not clear-cut, for in many legal relationships the State and its agencies are subject to the ordinary principles of private law such as in matters of contract or property.

Public enterprise is a term which is seldom defined in Great Britain. It is often used as a synonym for nationalized industries, but the domain of public enterprise is larger than this, since it includes activities of local government, such as public transport services, and of executive agencies (created by central government), for example, in regional development. On the other hand public enterprise is smaller than the public sector, since the latter includes the civil service, the armed forces and the greater part of the education and health services.

The distinguishing characteristics of public enterprise, which set it apart from private enterprise and from the public sector, are twofold. The first is that public enterprise is either owned by or responsible to central or local government, and the second is that charges are made for the goods or services, and these charges are related broadly to the costs of their provision. The latter is often a matter of degree.

Just as the boundary of public enterprise is difficult to define with precision, there are no clear principles which determine why some industries in Great Britain are public enterprises while others remain as private enterprises. Public enterprises have been created for a variety of reasons. Some were created for rea-

reich zu betrachten sind. Die öffentlichen Unternehmen wurden aus einer Vielzahl von Anlässen heraus gegründet. Manche wurden aus weltanschaulichen Gründen von Regierungen der Arbeiterpartei gegründet; das geschah insbesondere in den Jahren 1945 bis 1950 und 1964 bis 1970. Beispielsweise wurden in den Jahren 1945 bis 1950 der Kohlenbergbau, die Stahlindustrie, die Gas- und Elektrizitätswirtschaft nationalisiert, wogegen konservative Regierungen seit 1979 Schritte der Privatisierung einiger staatlicher Unternehmen wie zum Beispiel der *Britoil* eingeleitet haben. Öffentliche Unternehmen haben sich in einigen Fällen aus traditionellen Staatsfunktionen heraus entwickelt, so aus der Post *(GPO)* in neue Bereiche hinein wie das Fernmeldewesen *(British Telecom)*. Manche öffentlichen Versorgungsunternehmen, die früher in kommunalem oder privatem Besitz waren, sind in öffentliches Eigentum überführt worden: Das geschah beispielsweise für die Gas- und Elektrizitätswirtschaft, die nationalisiert wurde, oder für die Regionalen Wasserämter, die im Rahmen öffentlicher Einrichtungen für bestimmte Gebiete bestehen. Andere öffentliche Unternehmen ergaben sich aus der Rationalisierung früher gemischtwirtschaftlicher oder kommunaler Tätigkeitsbereiche wie zum Beispiel des öffentlichen Autobusverkehrs. Weitere öffentliche Unternehmen sind entstanden aus Sanierungsbemühungen des Staates für bestimmte Wirtschaftsberichte, so zum Beispiel *British Shipbuilders* und *British Leyland* (die Automobilfirma), während der Staat Exekutiveinrichtungen geschaffen hat, die der Durchführung einer bestimmten politischen Zielsetzung entsprechen, wie etwa die *Scottish Development Agency* und die *Welsh Development Agency* (zur Förderung der wirtschaftlichen Entwicklung in diesen Ländern). Manche Unternehmen sind gegründet worden, um in einer quasi-kommerziellen Atmosphäre tätig zu werden, aber im Rahmen eng umgrenzter nationaler Interessen; das geschah beispielsweise für *British Nuclear Fuels* im Bereich der zivilen Kernenergiewirtschaft. Der Staat hat weiter Finanzierungseinrichtungen im Rahmen des öffentlichen Sektors geschaffen, um bestimmte Lücken in der Finanzierung für den privaten Sektor zu füllen; das gilt beispielsweise für die *British Technology Group,* die die Forschung und Entwicklung fördern soll.

Wenn es bereits schwierig ist, die öffentliche Wirtschaft definitionsgemäß abzugrenzen, dann ist es ebenso schwierig, ihren Beitrag zur Produktion und zur Beschäftigung in der nationalen Gesamtwirtschaft quantitativ zu ermitteln. Im Jahre 1980 erstellte der öffentliche Sektor insgesamt rund 29% der Güter und Leistungen in der britischen Wirtschaft. Davon hatten die öffentlichen Unternehmen, die als öffentliche Körperschaften konstituiert sind *(public corporations),* 11% aufzuweisen. Wenn man dann noch das öffentliche Gesundheitswesen, die kommunalen Erziehungs- und Bildungseinrichtungen, die öffentliche Verwaltung und die Verteidigung von den 29% abrechnet, dann bleibt ein ungefährer Anteil der öffentlichen Wirtschaft an der Gesamtproduktion von 15%, das heißt nur 4% gehört zu den öffentlichen Unternehmen außerhalb des Sektors der *public corporations*. Die Ziffern für die Beschäftigungssituation im Jahre

sons of political philosophy by Labour Governments, especially those of 1945–50 and 1964–70; for example the period 1945–50 saw the nationalization of coal, steel, rail, gas and electricity, while the Conservative Governments since 1979 have taken steps to privatize some State industries e.g. Britoil. Public enterprises have in some cases developed from traditional State functions such as postal services (the GPO) into new fields such as telecommunications (British Telecom). Some public utilities formerly in municipal or private ownership have been taken into public ownership as part of nationalized industries, such as gas and electricity or as constituents of area authorities e.g. Regional Water Authorities. Others have emerged from the rationalization of formerly mixed private sector or municipal activities e.g. urban bus transport. Several enterprises have arisen from economic salvage operations on the part of the State, e.g. British Shipbuilders, British Leyland (cars), while the State has established executive agencies to achieve particular policy aims e.g. Scottish Development Agency and Welsh Development Agency (to promote economic development within these countries). Some enterprises have been formed to operate in a quasi-commercial environment, but within a narrowly defined national interest, for example British Nuclear Fuels in the civil nuclear field. The State has also created public sector financial institutions to meet perceived gaps in private sector provision e.g. British Technology Group to support research and development.

Just as it is difficult to define public enterprise, so it is difficult to quantify its contribution to national output and employment. In 1980 the public sector as a whole produced about 29% of the output of goods and services in the economy. Public corporations accounted for 11% of the 29%. If public health services, local authority education services, public administration and defence are removed, an approximate measure of public enterprise output is around 15%, i.e. only 4% comes from outside the public corporations. The figures for employment for 1981 broadly confirm these estimates. Employment in the public sector as a whole is about 31% of all employment, of which central government accounts for 10%, local authorities 13% and public corporations 8%. Removing those employed in the armed forces, the non-industrial civil ser-

1981 bestätigen in großen Zügen diese Schätzungen. Die Zahl der Arbeitskräfte im öffentlichen Sektor insgesamt macht etwa 31% der Gesamtbeschäftigtenzahl aus; davon entfallen auf die Zentralverwaltung etwa 10%, auf die örtlichen Gebietskörperschaften 13% und auf die öffentlichen Körperschaften 8%. Wenn man von den 23%, die für die zentralen und örtlichen Gebietskörperschaften tätig sind, diejenigen abrechnet, die in den Streitkräften, im nichtgewerblichen öffentlichen Verwaltungsdienst, im Gesundheitswesen und im Erziehungs- und Bildungswesen auf kommunaler Ebene tätig sind, und dann den Rest der Ziffer für die öffentlichen Körperschaften zurechnet, ergibt sich eine Gesamtziffer von etwa 17% als Anteil der Beschäftigten in der öffentlichen Wirtschaft an der Gesamtbeschäftigtenzahl.

2.2 Die Organisation der öffentlichen Wirtschaft

Die vorherrschende Rechtsform für die wichtigsten Bereiche der öffentlichen Wirtschaft ist die öffentliche Körperschaft *(public corporation);* aber es gibt auch andere Rechtsformen für andere Bereiche der öffentlichen Wirtschaft, so etwa staatliche Regiebetriebe *(Government Trading Funds)* und kommunale Unternehmen.

Wie auch zahlreiche andere britische Einrichtungen entstand die öffentliche Körperschaft als Reaktion auf besondere Gegebenheiten. Ihre Ursprünge lassen sich bis in die zwanziger Jahre hinein verfolgen; aber erst in den vierziger Jahren gewann die öffentliche Körperschaft an Bedeutung, denn damals wurde die Struktur der nationalisierten Unternehmen in dieser Rechtsform festgelegt. Die Bezeichnung *public corporation* ist unmittelbar mit dem Namen von Herbert Morrison verbunden, ihrem führenden politischen Vorkämpfer, und man sagt daher, die öffentlichen Körperschaften seien nach den „Morrisonschen Prinzipien" organisiert und sollten „auf den Abstand der Armeslänge" entfernt von den staatlichen Instanzen tätig werden *(at arm's length).*

Nach diesen Grundsätzen ist es unangebracht, große Wirtschaftskomplexe wie Ministerien zu betreiben, mit all der Vorsicht und Zurückhaltung, wie sie für solche typisch ist. Für die Geschäftsführung solcher Unternehmen bedarf es eben eines hohen Grades an Unternehmungsgeist und Flexibilität. Öffentliche Körperschaften sind öffentliche Geschäftsbetriebe, die einen erheblichen Grad finanzieller Unabhängigkeit gegenüber den staatlichen Instanzen aufzuweisen haben. Ihr Vorstand mag zwar von den jeweiligen Ministern oder vom Parlament ernannt werden, behält aber im Prinzip freie Hand, um in den täglichen Geschäftsoperationen der Unternehmen nach Belieben zu verfahren; dabei unterliegt er lediglich allgemeinen Anweisungen seitens des zuständigen Fachministers im Hinblick auf die Wahrnehmung und Durchführung seiner Aufgaben bezüglich von Angelegenheiten, die nach Ansicht des Ministers das öffentliche Interesse berühren. Die Minister erhalten auch spezifische Vollmachten gegen-

vice, the health services and local authority education services reduces the overall figure to around 17%.

2.2 Organization of Public Enterprises

The predominant method of management for the most important forms of public enterprise is the public corporation, but administrative structures for other forms of public enterprise include government trading funds and municipal enterprises.

Like many British institutions the public corporation grew in response to particular circumstances. Its origins can be traced back to the 1920s but the public corporation came into prominence in the late 1940s when the industries nationalized at that time were given this structure. Associated with the name of Herbert Morrison, their major political protagonist, public corporations are said to be organized on "Morrisonian" principles and to operate "at arm's length" from the government.

According to these principles, it is inappropriate to run large industries as departments of state with the caution and circumspection typical of such departments. A high degree of enterprise and flexibility is needed for the conduct of their business. Public corporations are public trading bodies with a substantial degree of financial independence from government. Whilst it may be appointed by Ministers or Parliament, the board of management is in principle free to do as it wishes in the day-to-day running of the industry, subject only to directions of a general character from the relevant government minister as to the exercise and performance of its functions in relation to matters appearing to the minister to affect the national interest. Ministers are also given specific powers over public corporations in matters of special importance such as capital expenditure.

über öffentlichen Körperschaften in Angelegenheiten, die von besonderer Bedeutung sind, wie beispielsweise Kapitalaufwendungen bzw. Investitionen.

Die Frage, wie weit die ministerielle Einmischung gehen darf, bildet einen ständigen Streitpunkt zwischen den Vorständen der öffentlichen Körperschaften und dem Staat. Bei verschiedenen Anlässen haben sich Minister formlos in die täglichen Geschäftsvorgänge der öffentlichen Körperschaften eingemischt, um bestimmte staatliche Zielsetzungen zu verfolgen, beispielsweise um im Rahmen der Inflationsbekämpfung die Preise niedrig zu halten. Die kommerzielle Leistungsfähigkeit der öffentlichen Körperschaft ist auf diese Weise erheblich beeinträchtigt worden, und da die betreffenden Anweisungen informellen Charakter trugen und keine allgemeinen Anweisungen waren, unterlagen sie auch nicht der Debatte im Parlament, wie das der Fall ist bei generellen Richtlinien, die ebenso wie die Geschäftsberichte der öffentlichen Körperschaften einer parlamentarischen Erörterung unterliegen dürfen. Im Jahre 1978 wurde in einem Weißbuch der Versuch unternommen, das Problem der ministeriellen Einmischung zu behandeln, indem man den Ministern die Vollmacht gab, dem Vorstand entweder generelle oder spezifische Anweisungen zu erteilen. Der Gedanke war dabei, daß damit die Rechenschaftslegung klarer gestaltet werden würde, indem formell und in aller Öffentlichkeit festgestellt werden würde, daß ein Minister dem betreffenden Vorstand bestimmte Pflichten auferlegt oder sich über dessen rein geschäftliche Überlegungen hinwegsetzt.

Die Unabhängigkeit der öffentlichen Körperschaften erstreckt sich auch auf den finanziellen Bereich; hier haben sie die Vollmacht zur Kreditaufnahme, innerhalb der vom Parlament vorgeschriebenen Grenzen, und sie haben weiter die Vollmacht zur Bildung ihrer Rücklagen. Mit diesem Charakterzug unterscheiden sich öffentliche Körperschaften von anderen Geschäftsbetrieben der Zentralregierung wie beispielsweise der Forstkommission *(Forestry Commission)* oder den staatlichen Arsenal- bzw. Rüstungsbestrieben *(armaments factories)* und von den kommunalen Unternehmen, denn diese erhalten ihre Finanzierungsmittel von den zuständigen öffentlichen Behörden und führen etwaige Überschüsse an diese ab.

Nach ihren Gründungsstatuten waren die öffentlichen Körperschaften in der Regel nur gehalten, ihre Aufwendungen mit den Erträgen zu decken über eine Reihe von Jahren hinweg, einschließlich der Abschreibungen auf der Basis von Anschaffungskosten. Die Zielsetzung der Unternehmen bestand nicht darin, daß sie Gewinne machen sollten, sondern darin, daß sie einem öffentlichen Zweck dienen und im besten Interesse der Nation tätig werden sollten, indem sie effizient, sparsam und zu angemessenen Preisen arbeiteten. Im Laufe der Zeit hat man erlebt, daß die öffentlichen Körperschaften einer strengeren finanziellen Disziplin unterworfen wurden. Zahlreiche Unternehmen gelangten nicht zur Kostendeckung, wobei die Zielsetzung der Kostendeckung als solche bedeutete, daß der Staat in einer Situation, in der die Wiederbeschaffungskosten normalerweise über die Anschaffungskosten der Anlagen hinausgingen, die Fi-

The extent of ministerial intervention has in practice been a source of friction between the boards of public corporations and the government. Ministers have on several occasions intervened informally in the day-to-day affairs of the corporations to further a general government objective e.g. to keep prices down as part of an anti-inflation policy. The commercial performance of the corporation has been impaired in this way, and since the instruction was informal and not of a general nature, it has not been subject to parliamentary debate, as occurs with general directives which, like the reports of corporations, may be subject to debate in Parliament. A White Paper of 1978 attempted to deal with the problem of ministerial intervention by allowing ministers the power to give a board either general or specific instructions, the idea being that this would clarify accountability by indicating formally and publicly when a minister imposed a duty on the board or over-ruled its commercial judgement.

The independence of public corporations also extends to financial matters, where they have the power to borrow, within limits laid down by Parliament, and to maintain their own reserves. This feature distinguishes public corporations from other central government trading bodies such as the Forestry Commission or the Royal Ordnance (armaments) Factories and from local authority enterprises, which obtain finance from and return any surpluses to their responsible public authority.

In their acts of establishment the public corporations were normally required only to pay their way out of revenue over a period of years, including depreciation on a historic cost basis. Their objective was not to make profits, but to pursue a public purpose operating to the best advantage of the nation by being efficient, economical and levying reasonable charges. The passage of time has seen the corporations subjected to tighter financial discipline. Many corporations failed to break even, while the objective of breaking even itself meant that in a situation where replacement costs normally exceeded historic costs for assets, the government had to find finance for capital expenditure, or the corporation had to borrow from the public, both of which could create complications for government control of the economy. By the late 1960s public corporations were being set target rates of return on their overall assets, though

nanzierungsmittel für die Kapitalaufwendungen (Ersatzinvestition) aufzubringen hatte, oder aber die Unternehmung mußte Kredite auf dem Kapitalmarkt aufnehmen. In beiden Fällen würden sich für die staatliche Kontrolle über die Gesamtwirtschaft Komplikationen ergeben haben. In den späten sechziger Jahren wurden den öffentlichen Körperschaften dann Ertragsziele in Form prozentualer Renditen auf ihre Gesamtanlagewerte vorgeschrieben, wenngleich diese Rendite je nach dem Unternehmen und je nach dem Zeitverlauf wechselte. Darüber hinaus unterlagen alle neuen Investitionsvorhaben einem Testdiskontsatz *(test discount rate – TDR)*, und nur diejenigen Vorhaben konnten verfolgt werden, die diesen Mindestertrag oder mehr erbrachten. In den Preisen für die betreffenden erstellten Güter oder Leistungen sollten die vollen Kosten für die Erstellung zum Ausdruck kommen, auf der Basis langfristiger Grenzkosten, in die Rücklagen für die Wiederbeschaffung der Anlagen und eine angemessene Verzinsung des Eigenkapitals einzukalkulieren wären.

Mit dem Weißbuch von 1978 wurden nun verschiedene Änderungen in dieses System eingefügt. Den Unternehmen wurden noch weiter finanzielle Ertragsziele vorgeschrieben, aber statt des Testdiskontsatzes wurde eine »erforderliche Ertragsrate« *(required rate of return – RRR)* von 5% real gerechnet auf ein neues Investitionsprogramm in seiner Gesamtheit angesetzt. Die Notwendigkeit einer Preiskalkulation zu langfristigen Grenzkosten wurde ebenfalls aufgegeben, und die Unternehmen erhielten freie Hand, ihre Preise nach den Marktgegebenheiten zu gestalten. Das finanzielle Ertragsziel, das über eine Fünfjahresperiode hinweg zu erreichen war, wurde ergänzt durch eine Finanzierungsbegrenzung für die Aufnahme von Fremdkapital *(external financing limit – EFL)* bezüglich der Aufnahme von Außenkrediten seitens einer Unternehmung. Da nun in den Depressionsbedingungen der frühen achtziger Jahre viele Unternehmen ihre finanziellen Ertragsziele nicht erreichen konnten, wurde die Finanzierungsbegrenzung *(EFL)* zum Hauptinstrument der Finanzkontrolle über öffentliche Unternehmen. Dies war sogar zutreffend für Unternehmen, die Gewinne abwarfen, denn diese mußten nicht nur eine Finanzierungsbegrenzung beachten (also die *EFL*), sondern hatten von Zeit zu Zeit auch Sonderabhebungen ihrer Gewinne zu erdulden oder wurden veranlaßt, Kredite zu tilgen, womit ihre Handlungsfreiheit eingeschränkt wurde. Vom Finanzministerium des Vereinigten Königreichs *(UK Treasury)* wurden Finanzierungsbegrenzungen *(EFLs)* eingeführt als Teil von Versuchen, die staatliche Kreditaufnahme *(public sector borrowing requirement – PSBR –* Kreditaufnahmebedarf des öffentlichen Sektors) möglichst niedrig zu halten, denn diese umfaßt auch die Fremdkapitalaufnahme seitens der öffentlichen Körperschaften bzw. Großunternehmen.

In den Fällen, wo öffentliche Unternehmen nicht den Charakter von öffentlichen Körperschaften haben und der Kontrolle der zentralstaatlichen Instanzen unterliegen, sind sie üblicherweise als Eigenbetriebe *(trading funds)* organisiert. Diese stehen effektiv unter der Kontrolle eines staatlichen Ministeriums, be-

this rate varied between corporations and over time. In addition all new investment projects were subject to a test discount rate (TDR) and only those projects were to go ahead which could earn this rate or better. The prices for the goods or services were to reflect the full cost of provision and relate to long run marginal costs, which were to include provision for replacement of assets and a satisfactory rate of return on capital employed.

The White Paper of 1978 introduced several changes. Corporations were still set overall financial targets, but the TDR gave way to a required rate of return (RRR) of 5% in real terms on a new investment programme as a whole. The requirement of long run marginal cost pricing was also abandoned, and corporations given freedom to price according to market conditions. The financial target to be attained over a five-year period has been supplemented by an external financing limit (EFL) on the funds a corporation may borrow from outside sources. With many industries failing to attain their financial targets in a depressed economy in the early 80s, the EFL has become the major financial control over public corporations. This has been true even of the profitable corporations which, in addition to having to observe an EFL, have from time to time been subject to ad hoc levies on their profits or been made to repay debt principal, thereby restricting their freedom of action. EFLs were introduced by the UK Treasury as part of an attempt to control the public sector borrowing requirement (PSBR) since this includes the public corporations' requirement for external funds.

Where public enterprises are not public corporations and are controlled by central government, they are usually organized as trading funds. These are effectively under the control of a government department, deriving their funds

kommen ihre Finanzmittel aus Zuweisungen des Finanzministeriums und führen etwaige Überschüsse an ihren jeweiligen öffentlichen Träger ab. Beispiele für solche staatlichen Eigenbetriebe sind die Königliche Münze *(Royal Mint)* und die Königlichen Arsenale bzw. Rüstungsfabriken *(Royal Ordnance Factories)*.

Die öffentlichen Unternehmen auf der örtlichen bzw. kommunalen Ebene sind in einer Weise organisiert, die diesen Eigenbetrieben *(trading funds)* ähnlich ist, denn sie bringen nicht selber ihr Kapital auf und führen etwaige Überschüsse an die örtliche Trägerkörperschaft ab, von der sie errichtet wurden, bzw. erhalten von dieser ihre Zuschüsse. Der Tätigkeitsbereich, den die örtlichen bzw. kommunalen Instanzen umfassen, ist jetzt in seinen Dimensionen geringer, als dies sich auf der kommunalen Ebene im neunzehnten Jahrhundert entwickelt hatte, denn viele der Tätigkeitsbereiche, die auf der lokalen Ebene zum Tragen kamen, zum Beispiel in der Gasversorgung, der Stromversorgung und im Krankenhauswesen sind von Unternehmen übernommen worden, die von den zentralstaatlichen Instanzen errichtet wurden, nämlich entweder von öffentlichen Körperschaften wie *British Gas* oder vom Nationalen Gesundheitsdienst *(National Health Service)*. Trotzdem wird noch eine Vielzahl von Unternehmungen auf der lokalen bzw. kommunalen Ebene von den örtlichen bzw. kommunalen Instanzen betrieben, auf der Grundlage freier Preisgestaltung.

Sehr wichtig ist hier die Wohnungswirtschaft, auf dem Wege über einen Wohnungsertragsfonds *(Housing Revenue Account)*. Historisch gesehen hat die Zentralregierung umfangreiche Zuschüsse zum Wohnungsbau geleistet, aber infolge von Kürzungen der staatlichen Subventionen betreiben die örtlichen bzw. kommunalen Instanzen ihre Wohnungswirtschaft mehr und mehr auf einer quasi-kommerziellen Basis.

Die meisten örtlichen bzw. kommunalen Behörden verfügen über direkte Arbeitsregiebetriebe *(Direct Labour Organizations – DLOs)* innerhalb ihrer Wohnungs- oder Straßenbauabteilungen, die bestimmte Reparaturarbeiten durchführen. An einigen Orten haben diese sich zu großen Baubetrieben ausgewachsen, die analog sind zu privaten Bau- und Konstruktionsfirmen. Mit dem Gesetz für örtliche Behörden, Bauplanung und Grundstücksverwaltung *(Local Government, Planning and Land Act,* 1980) wurden Vorschriften eingeführt, mit denen diese Regiebetriebe *(DLOs)* in einer eigenbetriebsähnlichen Form eingeordnet wurden.

In den größeren Stadtkomplexen bestehen kommunale Autobusunternehmen. Viele Städte haben daneben noch Großhandels- und Einzelhandels-Marktbetriebe und Hafenanlagen, die auf der Grundlage von Eigenbetrieben gehalten sind. Regionale Flughäfen werden vielfach auch als Eigenbetriebe verwaltet, und zwar von Zweckverbänden *(joint boards)* örtlich-kommunaler Instanzen. Einige Gemeinderäte sind durch örtliche Gesetzesregelungen, die vom Parlament angenommen wurden, dazu bevollmächtigt, Liegenschaften und Grundstücke auf kommerzieller Basis (als »Grundstückskörperschaften« – *»corporate estate«)* zu verwalten.

from Exchequer grants and returning any surpluses to their parent body. Examples of trading funds are the Royal Mint and Royal Ordnance Factories.

The public enterprises of local authorities are organized in a manner similar to trading funds, since they do not raise capital themselves and return any surpluses to (or receive subsidies from) the local authority by which they were established. The range of activities offered by local authorities is now smaller than it was as local government developed in the nineteenth century, since many of the activities introduced at the local level, e.g. gas, electricity, hospitals, have been taken over by enterprises established by central government, either public corporations like British Gas or the National Health Service. Local authorities do, however, still operate a large number of local services on a pricing basis.

Most significant is housing, through a Housing Revenue Account. Historically, central government has supplied large subsidies for dwelling construction but as a result of cutbacks in government subsidy, local authorities are increasingly operating housing stock on a quasi-commercial basis.

Most local authorities have direct labour organizations (DLOs) within their housing or highways departments to carry out repairs functions. In some places, these have grown into large construction forces, analogous to private building and civil engineering firms. The Local Government, Planning and Land Act 1980 introduced regulations to place DLOs on a proper trading fund basis.

Municipal bus undertakings exist in the larger urban areas of Britain and many towns operate wholesale and retail markets and harbour facilities on a trading fund basis. Regional airports are often run as trading funds by joint boards of local authorities. Some councils have powers under local acts of Parliament to operate holdings of land and property on a commercial ("corporate estate") basis.

Zu den Bereichen, die gewöhnlich als »Dienstleistungsbetriebe« betrachtet werden, tatsächlich aber auf der Grundlage einer Preiskalkulation betrieben werden seitens der örtlich-kommunalen Instanzen, gehören auch Schwimmbäder und Sporthallen, Theater, Kraftfahrzeugparks und Kombinationsbetriebe (*»assembly rooms«*).

Alle vorgenannten Arten von Betrieben werden von den örtlich-kommunalen Instanzen auf der Grundlage spezifischer gesetzlicher Vollmachten gehalten. Darüber hinaus ist es nach § 137 des Kommunalgesetzes von 1972 *(Local Government Act)* zulässig, daß Aufwendungen für nicht näher spezifierte Aufgaben bis zur Grenze eines Anteils am Grundsteueraufkommen *(rate product)* von 2 *Pence* vorgenommen werden können. Von dieser allgemeinen Vollmacht machen die örtlich-kommunalen Behörden mehr und mehr Gebrauch, um damit in den Bereich der wirtschaftlichen Entwicklung auf quasi-kommerzieller Basis einzusteigen.

Zweckverbände bzw. örtliche Betriebe sind in Teilen Englands gebildet worden, um kommunal-örtliche Finanzmittel in die Unterstützung wirtschaftlicher Vorhaben in den betreffenden Räumen zu schleusen.

Neben öffentlichen Körperschaften, Eigenbetrieben der zentralstaatlichen Instanzen und örtlich-kommunalen Unternehmen ist nun auch noch darauf hinzuweisen, daß die Zentralregierung Anteile an Aktiengesellschaften bzw. Gesellschaften mit beschränkter Haftung im Besitz hat, die zu den Kapitalgesellschaften des Landes gehören. Manchmal gehört die ganze Gesellschaft dem Staat; vielfach handelt es sich hier um Sanierungsoperationen wie beispielsweise bei der Automobilfirma *British Leyland*. Manchmal handelt es sich dagegen um Beteiligungen an gemischtwirtschaftlichen Unternehmen; das am besten bekannte Beispiel ist *British Petroleum – BP*.

Außerdem lassen sich viele sogenannte *QUANGOS (quasi-autonomous non-governmental organizations or agencies* = quasi-autonome nichtstaatliche Organisationsgebilde – hier setzt sich die aktuelle Bezeichnung »nichtministerielle öffentliche Einrichtung« durch) als öffentliche Unternehmen betrachten. Ihre Vorstände werden normalerweise von der Regierung ernannt; diese dürfte in der Regel auch einen Gutteil ihrer Operationen finanzieren. Solche *quangos* können Aufgaben wahrnehmen, die denen der Zentralregierung ähnlich sind; aber ihre Arbeitnehmer werden nicht als öffentliche Bedienstete angesehen. Beispiele für *quangos* dieser Art, von denen es insgesamt mehr als 400 gibt, sind die *Countryside Commission* (Kommission zur Landschaftspflege), die *Tourist Boards,* der Rat für nationale akademische Grade *(Council for National Academic Awards)* und die Kommission für Monopole und Fusionen *(Monopolies and Mergers Commission)*.

Among activities which are commonly perceived as "services" but are in fact operated on a pricing basis by local authorities are swimming baths and sports halls, theatres, car parks and assembly rooms.

All the preceeding kinds of enterprise are run by local authorities on the basis of specific statutory powers. In addition, Section 137 of the Local Government Act 1972 permits expenditure for unspecified purposes up to the limit of a 2p.-rate product. This general power is increasingly being used by local authorities to enter the field of economic development on a quasi-commercial basis.

Local enterprise boards have been set up in parts of England to channel local government funds into support of economic ventures in the area.

In addition to public corporations, trading funds of central government and local authority enterprises, the central government also owns shares in limited companies which are included in the company sector of the economy. Sometimes the company is owned outright, often as a result of a rescue operation e.g. British Leyland, and sometimes ownership is partial, the best known example being British Petroleum.

QUANGOS (quasi-autonomous non governmental agencies), for which the preferred official usage is becoming non-departmental public body, can also be considered as public enterprises. Their governing body will normally be appointed by the Government, which is also likely to finance part of their operations. Quangos may perform tasks similar to central government but their employees are not regarded as civil servants. Examples of quangos, of which there are over 400, are the Countryside Commission, Tourist Boards, the Council for National Academic Awards and the Monopolies and Mergers Commission.

2.3 Die Ausübung der parlamentarischen Kontrolle über öffentliche Unternehmen

Die Minister können den öffentlichen Körperschaften allgemeine oder spezifische Anweisungen erteilen, aber die Möglichkeiten für das Parlament zur Erörterung und Beeinflussung der Politik öffentlicher Körperschaften sind begrenzt. Das ist eine Situation, die manche als durchaus wünschenswert im Interesse einer Wahrung der Unabhängigkeit der Unternehmensgebilde ansehen; andere betrachten sie aber als keineswegs wünschenswert, weil sich daraus eine nur begrenzte Rechenschaftslegung ergibt. Das Parlament diskutiert die Jahresberichte der öffentlichen Körperschaften, wenn diese dem Parlament vorgelegt werden, und einzelne Mitglieder des Parlaments können zu jeder Zeit parlamentarische Anfragen generellen Charakters den für die einzelnen öffentlichen Körperschaften zuständigen Ministern vorlegen.

Der Präsident des Rechnungshofs *(Comptroller and Auditor General)*, der von der Krone ernannt wird, mit seinem Stab von mehr als 600 Mitarbeitern im Nationalen Rechnungshof *(National Audit Office)* prüft die Aufwendungen der zentralstaatlichen Instanzen. Vollmachten für eine Prüfung des Rechnungswesens öffentlicher Unternehmen sind für den Rechnungshof nur dann gegeben, wenn eine öffentliche Körperschaft Finanzmittel – beispielsweise in Form von Subventionen – von den zentralstaatlichen Instanzen erhält, denn sonst wird das Rechnungswesen solcher Unternehmen in der Regel von privaten Wirtschaftsprüfern überprüft. Im Unterhaus *(House of Commons)* gibt es allerdings einen Ausschuß für öffentliche Rechnungslegung *(Public Accounts Committee – PAC)*, der im Jahre 1861 gebildet wurde und den ältesten Sonderausschuß *(select committee)* des Parlaments darstellt; dieser Ausschuß arbeitet eng mit dem Präsidenten des Rechnungshofs zusammen. Der Ausschuß überprüft die Rechnungslegung, die dem Parlament unterbreitet wird. Seine Tätigkeit stellt nicht lediglich eine Untersuchung spezifischer vergangener Ereignisse dar, sondern kann auch die Form zukunftsorientierter Untersuchungen annehmen, die einen Einfluß auf die Politik der Regierungen ausüben können.

Das Parlament kann auch noch aus einer anderen Richtung her einen gewissen Einfluß auf die öffentlichen Körperschaften ausüben, denn seit 1979 gibt es insgesamt 12 Sonderausschüsse *(select committees)*, die jeweils einem bestimmten Ministerium zugeordnet sind und die bevollmächtigt sind, die Aufwendungen, die Verwaltung und die Politik der wichtigsten Ministerien und der ihnen zugeordneten öffentlichen Einrichtungen zu untersuchen.

Der Einfluß, den das Parlament auf diesen Wegen über die Ausschüsse geltend machen kann, macht sich allerdings bestenfalls nur indirekt bemerkbar. Diese Ausschüsse vermögen die ministeriellen Instanzen zu einer Überprüfung ihrer jeweiligen Politik veranlassen oder die jeweils am Ruder befindliche Regierung dazu zu bringen, ihre Auffassungen über die zu verfolgende Politik besser klarzulegen. Ihre wertvollste Funktion besteht wahrscheinlich darin, daß

2.3 Parliamentary Control over Public Enterprises

While government ministers may give public corporations general or specific instructions, the opportunities for Parliament to debate and influence the policy of public corporations are limited, a situation which some see as desirable for the commercial independence of the organizations and others see as undesirable because of consequent limited accountability. Parliamentary debates take place on the annual reports of public corporations when they are laid before Parliament, and individual members of Parliament can at any time ask Parliamentary questions of a general nature of ministers responsible for particular corporations.

The Comptroller and Auditor General, who is appointed by the Crown, and his staff of over 600 in the National Audit Office audit central government expenditure. The power of the Office to examine the accounts of public corporations applies only if a public corporation is in receipt of finance, for example subsidies, from central government, for otherwise the accounts of public corporations are prepared by private auditors. The Public Accounts Committee (PAC), established in 1861, is the senior select committee of the House of Commons and works closely with the Comptroller and Auditor General. The PAC examines accounts laid before Parliament. Its activities represent not just an inquest into specific past events but can take the form of forward-looking enquiries which can influence government policy.

Parliament can also exercise some influence over public corporations from another direction, for since 1979 there have been 12 departmentally related select committees, which are empowered to examine the expenditure, administration and policy of the principal government departments and their associated public bodies.

The influence of Parliament by means of these committees is at best indirect. They may cause government departments to review their policies or cause the government of the day to set out its views on policy more explicitly. Their most valuable function is probably to supply information for the use of members and to help in the development of an informed body of opinion outside the government and civil service.

sie Informationen zur Verwendung für die Parlamentarier beschaffen können, die in den Ausschüssen sitzen, und daß sie dabei mithelfen, daß eine gutorientierte Meinungsbildung außerhalb der Regierung und der Verwaltung zustande kommt.

Die staatliche – wenn auch nicht die parlamentarische – Einflußnahme auf die öffentlichen Körperschaften wurde im Jahre 1980 ausgeweitet, als die Kommission für Monopole und Fusionen die Möglichkeit zugestanden bekam, Untersuchungen über die Effizienz nationalisierter Unternehmen und einiger anderer öffentlicher Unternehmen vorzunehmen. Derartige Untersuchungen finden allerdings nur auf Veranlassung eines Ministers statt.

Die Zentralregierung versorgt normalerweise die örtlich-kommunalen Instanzen mit etwa der Hälfte bzw. einem Drittel der Einnahmen der letzteren, durch einen Zuschlag zum Grundsteueraufkommen *(rate support grant)*, wobei ein Teil dieser Zuwendungen von den örtlich-kommunalen Instanzen für den Betrieb öffentlicher Unternehmen verwendet wird. Da die Rechnungslegung der örtlich-kommunalen Instanzen von der Prüfungskommission für örtliche Behörden *(Audit Commission for Local Government)* überprüft wird, ist das Parlament in der Lage, daß es über die Ministerien Geld zur Verfügung stellt, ohne daß es imstande wäre, darüber Bescheid zu wissen, wie diese Gelder verwendet werden, denn der Rechnungshof überprüft nicht die Ausgaben der örtlich-kommunalen Instanzen.

Die konservativen Regierungen der frühen achtziger Jahre haben nun Versuche unternommen, den Umfang der Ausgaben der örtlich-kommunalen Behörden unter ihre Kontrolle zu bringen. Das geschah teilweise aus ideologischen Gründen, denn viele der örtlichen bzw. kommunalen Instanzen mit hohen Ausgaben waren in den Händen der Arbeiterpartei. Teilweise geschah dies aber auch aus der Überzeugung heraus, daß eine leistungsfähige Volkswirtschaft einen schmaleren staatlichen Sektor voraussetze. Die Zentralregierung hat sich um die Erreichung dieses Zieles in der Weise bemüht, daß sie die angeblich allzu ausgabefreudigen großstädtischen Gesamtkommunalräte abschaffte und ein »Abkappen« der Grundsteuererhebung vornahm. Der letztere Vorgang setzte voraus, daß eine bestimmte Zahl für die Ausgabe einer örtlich-kommunalen Instanz angesetzt wurde und gleichzeitig eine Obergrenze für die Grundsteuererhebung seitens der örtlich-kommunalen Instanz vorgeschrieben wurde. Ein paradoxes Ergebnis des Versuchs der Regierung, die Londoner zentrale Kommunalinstanz unter Kontrolle zu bringen, war eine zusätzliche Nationalisierung, denn an die Stelle von London-Transport – früher unter dem Rat von Groß-London – trat *London Regional Transport,* eine nur öffentliche Unternehmung, die der Aufsicht durch den Staatssekretär für Verkehr unterliegt.

Government though not parliamentary influence over public corporations was extended in 1980 when the Monopolies and Mergers Commission was allowed to undertake efficiency investigations into nationalized industries and certain other public corporations. Such investigations take place only at the instigation of a Minister.

Central government has typically supplied local government with anything from one half to two thirds of the latter's revenue through the rate support grant, some of which will be used by local government to run public enterprises. Since local government accounts are audited by the Audit Commission for Local Government, Parliament is in the position of supplying money via government departments without being in the position of fully knowing its use, since the Comptroller and Auditor General does not examine the expenditures of local authorities.

The Conservative governments of the early 1980's have been involved in attempts to control the extent of local government expenditure partly on ideological grounds, since many of the high-spending local governments have been Labour controlled, and partly from the belief that an efficient economy requires a smaller government sector. Central government has endeavoured to do this by abolishing the allegedly spendthrift metropolitan councils and by introducing "rate-capping". The latter process involves a figure for the expenditure of a local government unit and also setting an upper limit to the rate (a local tax levied on property) which the local government may levy. One paradoxical outcome of the central government's attempt to control local government in London has been the extension of nationalization, for London Transport, formerly run by Greater London Council, has been replaced by London Regional Transport, a non-departmental public body, reporting to the Secretary of State for Transport.

2.4 Die öffentliche Wirtschaft und der Verbraucher

Die Interessen der Verbraucher gegenüber den öffentlichen Unternehmen werden auf zweierlei Weise sichergestellt und wahrgenommen: Die erste Methode ist sehr indirekt und erfolgt eben dadurch, daß der Verbraucher gleichzeitig Wähler ist und in nationalen wie in kommunalen Wahlen für die Partei stimmen kann, deren Politik gegenüber den öffentlichen Unternehmen seiner eigenen Auffassung am ehesten entspricht. Die zweite Methode kommt über Verbraucher- und beratende Ausschüsse zum Tragen.

Für jeden nationalisierten Wirtschaftsbereich besteht mindestens ein solcher Beirat, dessen Mitglieder durch den zuständigen Minister ernannt werden. Diese Mitglieder sind repräsentativ sowohl für die Nutzer der Güter oder Leistungen, um die es hier geht, als auch für die Zulieferer. Der Beirat kann dem Minister gegenüber Bericht erstatten über etwelche Mängel seitens der betreffenden Unternehmung, und der Minister kann dann eine Anweisung an diese erlassen. Die Beiräte erstatten alljährlich Bericht an die Minister, und diese Berichte werden dem Parlament vorgelegt. Auch Einzelpersonen können Fragen oder Beschwerden bei den Beiräten vorbringen. Die Beiräte sind manchmal sehr effizient bei der Änderung der Politik der betreffenden Unternehmung oder sogar der Regierung; diese Effizienz kommt vielfach zum Tragen auf dem Wege über die Publizität, die ihre Tätigkeit oder ihre Berichte in der Presse oder im Rundfunk finden. Neuere Beispiele für ihre Einflußnahme finden sich im Bereich des Fernmeldewesens, wo bestimmte geplante Gebührenerhöhungen reduziert wurden.

2.4 Public Enterprise and the Consumer

The interests of the consumer vis-à-vis public enterprises are safeguarded and promoted in two main ways. The first is very indirect in that if the consumer is an elector, he may vote in national or local elections for the party whose policy towards public enterprise is nearest to his own views. The second is through consumers' and consultative councils.

Each nationalized industry has at least one such council, whose members are appointed by the relevant Minister. The members are representative of both the users of the goods or service and of the supplier. The council may report to the Minister on any deficiency on the part of the corporation and the Minister may issue a direction to the corporation. The councils produce annual reports to Ministers and these are laid before Parliament. Individuals may raise issues or complaints with the councils. The councils are sometimes effective in modifying corporation or government policy, often because of the publicity which their actions or reports receive in the press or radio. Recent examples of their influence can be seen in the telephone service, where some proposed price increases were reduced.

3. Beispiele für Privatisierung

Seit ihrer Übernahme der Regierung im Mai 1979 haben die Konservativen unter Mrs. Thatcher eine Politik des Verkaufs von Teilen der öffentlichen Wirtschaft an die Privatwirtschaft verfolgt, die generell als Privatisierungspolitik bezeichnet wird. Die Unternehmen, die privatisiert worden sind, sind unten aufgeführt, zusammen mit drei anderen, die bis 1987 privatisiert werden sollen.

Name in öffentlicher Hand	Name nach Privatisierung	Art der Privatisierung	Jahr
British Petroleum	British Petroleum	Staatsanteil verringert (stufenweise) von 51 auf etwa 31%	1979 und 1983
International Computers Limited	International Computers Limited	Staat verkaufte 25% des Holding-Anteils	1979
Fairey Aviation	Fairey Aviation	Verkauf der *NEB*-Gesellschaft	1980
Ferranti	Ferranti	Staat verkaufte 50% des Holding-Anteils	1980
British Aerospace	British Aerospace	Staatsanteil 1981 verringert von 100% auf 48% und verbleibende Aktien 1985 veräußert	1981 und 1985
Prestcold	Prestcold	Verkauf von Teilen von *British Leyland*	1981
National Freight Corporation	National Freight Corporation	Verkauf an Management und Personal	1981
Cable and Wireless	Cable and Wireless	Staatsanteil verringert von 100% auf 49%	1981
Radiochemical Centre	Amersham International	Verkauf des vollen Staatsanteils	1982

Name in öffentlicher Hand	Name nach Privatisierung	Art der Privatisierung	Jahr
British National Oil Corp.	Britoil	*BNOC* verkaufte Teil seiner Vermögenswerte zur Bildung einer Erdölgesellschaft. *BNOC* besteht daneben weiter	1982
British Transport Holdings	Verschiedene	Hotels verkauft an Private	1982
Associated British Ports	Associated British Ports	Staatsanteil verringert von 100% auf 48%	1983
British Gas Corporation	Enterprise Oil PLC	Die Nordseeanteile von *British Gas* verkauft	1984
British Gas Corporation	Dorset Group	Das Erdölfeld *Wytch Farm* auf dem britischen Festland verkauft	1984
Jaguar Cars	Jaguar PLC	Verkauf von Teilen von *British Leyland*	1984
British Telecom	British Telecom	Verkauf von 50% der Stammaktien	1984
Privatisierung vorgesehen			
1. British Airways			1987
2. British Gas			1986
3. British Airports Authority	British Airports PLC		1987

3. Examples of Privatization

Since obtaining office in May 1979 the Conservative governments under Mrs. Thatcher have adopted a policy of selling off parts of the public sector to the private sector, a process commonly known as privatization. The enterprises which have been privatized are listed below, as are three which are expected to be privatized by 1987.

Name in Public Ownership	Name after Privatization	Nature of Privatization	Year
British Petroleum	British Petroleum	State holdings reduced in stages from 51 to about 31%	1979 and 1983
International Computers Limited	International Computers Limited	State sold 25% holding	1979
Fairey Aviation	Fairey Aviation	Selling of NEB company	1980
Ferranti	Ferranti	State sold 50% holding	1980
British Aerospace	British Aerospace	State holding reduced from 100 to 48% in 1981 and remaining shares sold off in 1985	1981 and 1985
Prestcold	Prestcold	Sale of part of British Leyland	1981
National Freight Corporation	National Freight Corporation	Sold to Management and Staff	1981
Cable and Wireless	Cable and Wireless	State holding reduced from 100 to 49%	1981
Radiochemical Centre	Amersham International	Sale of entire State holding	1982

Name in Public Ownership	Name after Privatization	Nature of Privatization	Year
British National Oil Corp.	Britoil	B.N.O.C. sold off part of its assets to form an oil company. B.N.O.C. continues to exist as well.	1982
British Transport Holdings	Various	Hotels sold to private owners	1982
Associated British Ports	Associated British Ports	State holding reduced from 100 to 48%	1983
British Gas Corporation	Enterprise Oil PLC	British Gas North Sea oil interests sold off	1984
British Gas Corporation	Dorset Group	British Gas onshore oil field Wytch Farm sold off	1984
Jaguar Cars	Jaguar PLC	Sale of part of British Leyland	1984
British Telecom	British Telecom	Sale of 50% of ordinary share capital	1984
Privatization Proposals Pending			
1. British Airways			1987
2. British Gas			1986
3. British Airports Authority	British Airports PLC		1987

57

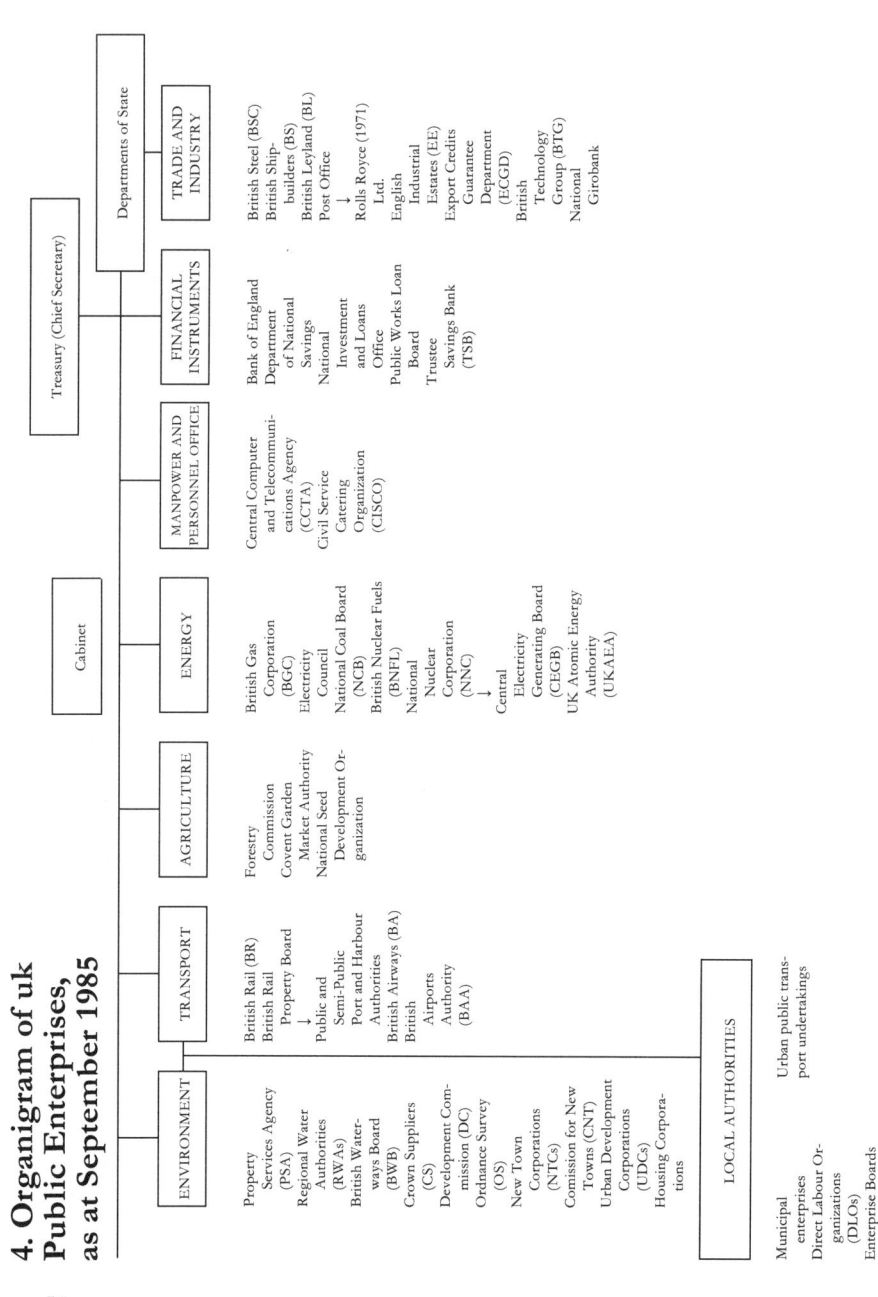

4. Organigram of UK Public Enterprises, as at September 1985

Cabinet

Treasury (Chief Secretary)

Departments of State

ENVIRONMENT

- Property Services Agency (PSA)
- Regional Water Authorities (RWAs)
- British Waterways Board (BWB)
- Crown Suppliers (CS)
- Development Commission (DC)
- Ordnance Survey (OS)
- New Town Corporations (NTCs)
- Comission for New Towns (CNT)
- Urban Development Corporations (UDCs)
- Housing Corporations

TRANSPORT

- British Rail (BR)
- British Rail Property Board ↓
- Public and Semi-Public Port and Harbour Authorities
- British Airways (BA)
- British Airports Authority (BAA)

AGRICULTURE

- Forestry Commission
- Covent Garden Market Authority
- National Seed Development Organization

ENERGY

- British Gas Corporation (BGC)
- Electricity Council
- National Coal Board (NCB)
- British Nuclear Fuels (BNFL)
- National Nuclear Corporation (NNC) ↓
- Central Electricity Generating Board (CEGB)
- UK Atomic Energy Authority (UKAEA)

MANPOWER AND PERSONNEL OFFICE

- Central Computer and Telecommunications Agency (CCTA)
- Civil Service Catering Organization (CISCO)

FINANCIAL INSTRUMENTS

- Bank of England
- Department of National Savings
- National Investment and Loans Office
- Public Works Loan Board
- Trustee Savings Bank (TSB)

TRADE AND INDUSTRY

- British Steel (BSC)
- British Shipbuilders (BS)
- British Leyland (BL)
- Post Office ↓
- Rolls Royce (1971) Ltd.
- English Industrial Estates (EE)
- Export Credits Guarantee Department (ECGD)
- British Technology Group (BTG)
- National Girobank

LOCAL AUTHORITIES

- Municipal enterprises
- Direct Labour Organizations (DLOs)
- Enterprise Boards
- Urban public transport undertakings

58

Departments of State						
	PAYMASTER GENERAL	HOME OFFICE	SCOTTISH OFFICE	WELSH OFFICE	DEFENCE	EMPLOYMENT
	Her Majesty's Stationery Office (HMSO)	British Broadcasting Corporation (BBC)	Scottish Development Agency (SDA)	Welsh Water Authority	Royal Ordnance Factories (ROFs)	Manpower Services Commission (MSC)
	Royal Mint	Independent Broadcasting Authority (IBA)	Scottish Bus Group	Welsh Development Agency (WDA)		Skillcentre Training Agency (STA)
			South of Scotland Electricity Board (SSEB)	Development Board for Rural Wales (DBRW)		Reemploy
			North of Scotland Hydroelectric Board (NSHEB)			
			Highlands & Islands Development Board (HIDB)			
			Scottish Special Housing Association (SSHA)			

ENTERPRISES WITH SUBSTANTIAL STATE HOLDINGS

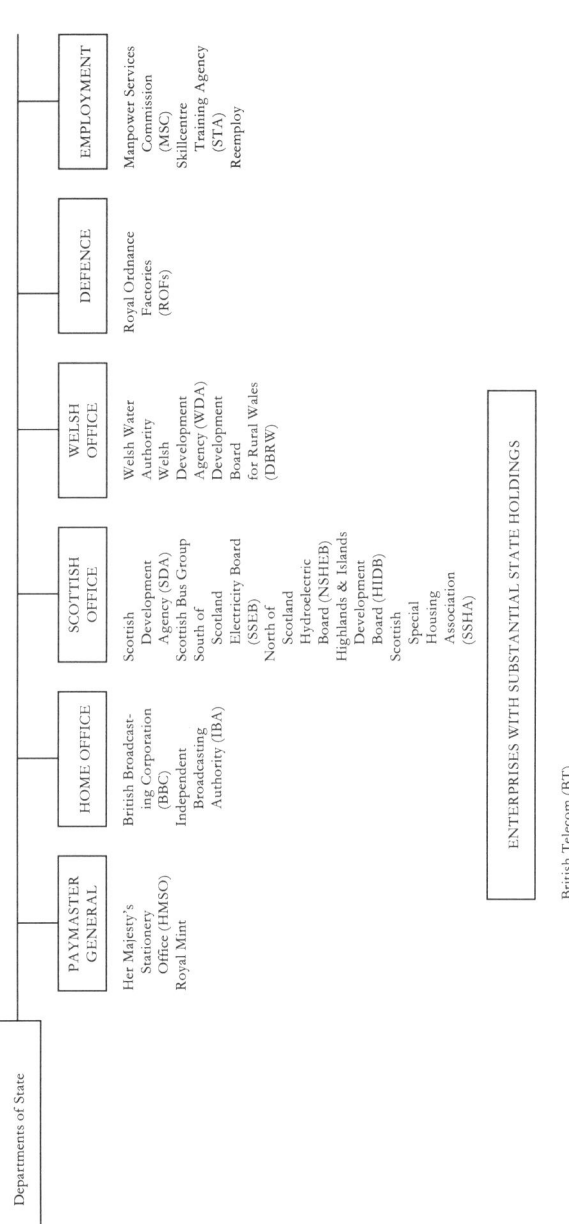

British Telecom (BT)
British Petroleum (BP)

5. Examples of Forms of Public Enterprises in the United Kingdom

Trading Fund — Royal Mint. Royal Ordnance Factories
Public Corporation — National Coal Board. British Rail
Statutory Undertakers — Severn Trent Water. Authority
Policy Based Agency — Scottish Development. Agency
Municipal Enterprise — Leicester City Transport
State Industrial Holdings — British Shipbuilders. British Petroleum

6. Begriffe zur öffentlichen Wirtschaft

6.1 Allgemeines

1 **öffentliche Wirtschaft** f.; **Eigenwirtschaft** f. **der öffentlichen Hand**
(öffentliche Wirtschaft; siehe Einleitung)

2 **öffentlicher Sektor** m.
(Begriff, wie in Großbritannien verwendet, umfaßt alle Gebietskörperschaften, das Gesundheits- und Bildungswesen und alle wirtschaftlichen Körperschaften und Versorgungsbetriebe der öffentlichen Hand)

3 **Gemeinwirtschaft** f.
(Gesamtheit solcher Wirtschaftsunternehmen der öffentlichen Hand oder der Genossenschaften [oder der Gewerkschaften], die im Dienste der Daseinsvorsorge ohne Gewinnprinzip tätig werden)

4 **gemeinwirtschaftlich; gemeinnützig**
(z.B. gemeinwirtschaftliche Zielsetzung)

5 **Gemeinwirtschaftlichkeit** f.

6 **Gemeinwirtschaftlichkeitswertung** f.

7 **öffentliches Interesse** n.; **Gemeinwohl** n.

8 **Sozialisierung** f.; **Vergesellschaftung** f. **(Kommunalisierung); Verstaatlichung** f.
(verstaatlichter Betrieb, kommunalisierter Betrieb, Gemeindebetrieb, Stadtwerke)

Terms relevant to the Public Sector of the Economy

General terms

= **public sector of the economy**

± **public sector**
(term used in Great Britain to encompass all central and local government bodies, the education and health services and all economic enterprises and statutory undertakings in public ownership)

± **not-for-profit enterprises**
(totality of those public enterprises or cooperatives [and – in Germany – trade-union enterprises] which operate on the principle of social responsibility without profit)

± **operating in the public interest without a profit motive**
(e.g. setting objectives in the public interest)

= **social accountability**

= **social audit**

= **public interest**

± **nationalization; social ownership**
(including municipal ownership); **taking into State ownership**
(State-owned enterprise, local authority enterprise, municipal enterprise)

9	Gemeineigentum n.	=	public ownership
10	Gemeinnützigkeit f. (eines Unternehmens)	±	orientation to public service (of an enterprise)
11	Gemeinwesen n.	=	society in a social (as opposed to legal) **sense;** any kind of less comprehensive **commonality**
12	Erstellung f. öffentlicher Leistungen	=	public provision
13	Funktionen fpl. öffentlicher Unternehmen (Steuerung; Modell; Preisregulierung; technische Neuerung; Entwicklung und Erschließung; Wettbewerb; wirtschaftliche Beherrschung)	=	purposes for which public enterprises are established (control of commanding heights of the economy; to set an example; influencing prices; technological innovation; development and planning; competition; sectoral dominance)
14	Richtlinienkompetenz f. (des Trägers gegenüber dem öffentlichen Unternehmen; s. Nr. 193)	=	power of direction (by the responsible body, to the public enterprise; s. No. 193)
15	öffentliches Unternehmen n. (steht als juristische Person des öffentlichen oder des privaten Rechts außerhalb der Gebietskörperschaft)	=	publicly-owned business (which can be incorporated under either public or private law separate from the territorial authority)
16	öffentliche Hand f.	±	public authorities
17	Daseinsvorsorge f.	±	practical social responsiblity in an active sense
18	soziale Verpflichtung f. ~ ~ von nationalisierten Unternehmen	= =	social obligations ~ ~ of nationalized industries
19	Verpflichtungen fpl. des öffentlichen Dienstes	=	public service obligations
20	Versorgung f. (z.B. mit Gas, Wasser, Strom, Verkehrsleistungen)	=	provision of public utilities (e.g. gas, water, electricity, transport undertakings)

21	Versorgungsauftrag m.	≠	tp.: specifically imposed public duty to supply a utility service, e.g. to certain areas
22	Versorgungswirtschaft f.	=	public utilities
23	Versorgungsnetz n.	=	supply network
	Versorgungsgebiet n.	=	supply area; area served
24	Verbindlichkeiten fpl.	=	liabilities (obligations)
25	≠ Üv.: Instrumentalunternehmen n. (Unternehmen, die für bestimmte politische Zwecke eingesetzt werden)		policy-based agencies (public bodies established to implement particular policy objectives [e.g. Scottish Development Agency, Merseyside Development Corporation])
26	Durchführungsorgane npl. (der Regierung)	±	executive agencies (of government)
27	**Fiskus** m. (als Vermögensverwaltung; als Steuerverwaltung)	=	**the State as financial body** (as Treasury; as Inland Revenue)
28	**Vermögensverwaltung** f.	±	**treasury function** (in an administration or enterprise); **administration of the assets of an undertaking**
29	**Wirtschaftsförderungsgesellschaft** f.	=	**economic development agency**
30	**Wirtschaftsförderung** f.	=	**promotion of economic development**
	regionale ~	=	regional ~ ~ ~ ~
	sektorale ~	=	sectoral ~ ~ ~ ~
31	**Gebietskörperschaft** f. (in Deutschland: Bund, Länder, Gemeindeverbände [z.B. Kreise], Gemeinden) In Großbritannien: In England und Wales gibt es	=	**territorial authority** (in Germany: Federal Government, *Laender,* associations of municipalities [e.g. districts], municipalities; in Great Britain: In England and Wales there are metro-

Stadtkreise, Grafschaften und Landkreise.
In Schottland bestehen Regionen und Kreise.)

politan districts, counties and shire districts.
In Scotland there are regions and districts.)

32 **Hilfsbetriebe** mpl. **der Verwaltung**

= auxiliary services of a public administration

33 **Leistungsverwaltung** f.
(Die öffentliche Verwaltung wird nicht nur ordnend, sondern auch leistend tätig, indem sie zur Erreichung wirtschafts-, gesellschafts-, sozial- oder kulturpolitischer Zwecke im öffentlichen Interesse für den Bürger bestimmte Leistungen erbringt oder Einrichtungen für die Öffentlichkeit bereitstellt. Sie dient damit der Daseinsvorsorge. Gegenstück: Hoheitsverwaltung)

= administration of public services
(Public administration not only has regulatory functions, but fulfils a positive role in the achievement of economic, social and cultural objectives for the public benefit, and the provision of facilities for public use. It thus demonstrates "practical social responsibility in an active sense", as opposed to the sovereign functions of the State.)

34 **Leistungsüberwachung** f.

= performance monitoring

35 **Gesamtleistung** f.

= overall performance

36 **Rechenschaftslegung** f.

= accountability of public sector

37 **Konzessionsvertrag** m.

(In Deutschland: gibt das ausschließliche Recht zur Benutzung von Gemeindeeigentum zur Verlegung von Leitungen oder Schienen;
in Großbritannien: Konzessionsträger dürfen zur Durchführung ihrer Aufgaben öffentlichen und privaten Grund und Boden ausgraben oder stören, z.B. zum Verlegen von Wasserleitungen.)

≠
tp.: concession contract
(in Germany: conveys exclusive right to use local authority property in order to divert or re-lay service ducts or tram lines;

in Great Britain: Statutory undertakers have a right to excavate or disturb public or private property in the exercise of their functions, e.g. re-laying water mains.)

38 **Konzession** f.
eine ~ erteilen für eine Leistung
eine ~ entziehen
Konzessionsgeber m.
Konzessionsnehmer m.
Konzessionsbetrieb m.

= concession
= to grant a ~ for the performance of a service
= to withdraw a ~
= concession giver
= concessionaire
= concessionary enterprise

63

39 **Konzessionsabgabe** f.

= **concessionary levy**

40 **Nutzungsüberlassung** f.;
Nutzungsverleihung f.;
Nutzungserlaubnis f.;
Gebrauchserlaubnis f.
(der für die Betriebsführung notwendigen Vermögenswerte durch die Gebietskörperschaft)

± **permission to use public resources**
(permission to use the resources made available by a public [local government] agency for carrying on the functions of a specific enterprise)

41 **Sondernutzung** f.
(Inanspruchnahme von öffentlichem Eigentum, die über den Gemeindegebrauch hinausgeht: z.B. von Straßen für die Verlegung von Leitungen und Schienen)

= **special use**
(use of a public facility for special purposes, e.g. of roads for laying service ducts)

42 **Genehmigung** f. einer **Sondernutzung**

= **approval of a special use**

43 **gesetzliches Leitungsmonopol** n.
(z.B. Gas, Elektrizität)

= **statutory supply monopoly**
(e.g. gas and electricity)

44 **Heimfallrecht** n.

= **law of reversion**

45 **Wegerecht** n.
(Enteignungsvollmachten gelten für Wegerecht und andere Rechte bei Überlandverlegungen z.B. von Elektrizitätskabeln.)

= **easement; wayleave**
(Compulsory purchase powers apply to easements and other rights over land e.g. for power cables.)

46 **Betriebsauflagen** fpl.
(z.B. eines Konzessionsnehmers)

= **operating conditions;**
~ **obligations**
(e.g. of a concessionaire)

47 **Kontrahierungszwang** m.;
Abschlußzwang m.;
Anschluß- und Versorgungspflicht f.
(Pflicht öffentlicher Monopolbetriebe zur Annahme eines Vertragsangebots)

= **compulsory connection obligation**
(obligation on public monopoly enterprises to accept a supply agreement [with a new user])

48 **Verbund** m.;
Verbundwirtschaft f.
(technisch-organisatorisches Mittel

± **horizontal integration**
(technical/organizational arrangements

	in der Versorgungs- und Verkehrswirtschaft zur Verbesserung der technischen Leistung: – Mehrere Kraftwerke z.B. werden mit mehreren Versorgungsgebieten verbunden. – Mehrere Verkehrsunternehmen stimmen Verkehrstarife und Fahrpläne ab.)		in public utility and transport undertakings to improve technical performance e.g. – local sharing between power grids; – common timetabling and fare structures in public transport)
49	Verbundvertrag m.	±	contract to secure (horizontal) integration
50	Hoheitsverwaltung f.; hoheitliche Verwaltung f.	=	the exercise of government as a regulatory function; sovereign functions of the State
	(insbesondere obrigkeitliche Verwaltung, die mit Geboten oder Verboten dem Bürger gegenübertritt; Gegenstück: Leistungsverwaltung)		(in particular, prescriptive administrative actions by the State authorities which present the citizen with orders or prohibitions; in contrast to community service function)
51	hoheitlich geregelte öffentliche Leistung f.	±	statutorily regulated public service
52	Privatwirtschaft f.	=	private economy
53	privater Sektor m. der Wirtschaft	=	private sector of the economy
54	Gewinnerzielungsabsicht f.	=	profit motive
55	Erwerbswirtschaft f.	=	profit-motivated economy
56	erwerbswirtschaftlich (Gegensatz: gemeinwirtschaftlich)	=	operating in the pursuit of profit (in contrast to: operating in the public interest without a profit motive)
57	marktwirtschaftliche Betriebsführung f.	=	to operate commercially
58	Betrieb m. gewerblicher Art (allgemeine Bezeichnung für wirtschaftliche Betriebe mit Ausnahme von Betrieben der Primärproduktion wie Landwirtschaft und Bergbau)	=	commercial or industrial enterprise (collective term for all economic enterprises, with the exception of those in primary production such as agriculture and mining)

59 **Privatisierung** f.
(öffentlicher Betriebe und Unternehmen; Gegensatz zu Sozialisierung, Verstaatlichung)

= **privatization**
(of public enterprises; in contrast to taking into social or State ownership)

60 **wirtschaften; eine Wirtschaftstätigkeit ausüben; sich wirtschaftlich betätigen**

= **to carry on a business**

61 **Auftragnehmer** m.

= **contractor**

62 **Leistungsfähigkeit** f. **des Betriebs**
(z.B. Erhaltung der technischen und wirtschaftlichen Leistungsfähigkeit)

= **viability of an enterprise**
(e.g. maintaining technical and economic viability)

63 **Subsidiaritätsprinzip** n.
(Grundsatz der Beschränkung der wirtschaftlichen Betätigung der öffentlichen Hand auf Bereiche fehlender oder unzureichender Privatinitiative)

± **principle of last resort**
(principle of limiting the economic activity of public authorities to areas in which private initiative is absent or insufficient)

64 **Rechtsform** f.; **Betriebsform** f.; **Unternehmensform** f.
(z.B. Wahl der Betriebsform aus steuerlichen Gründen)

= **legal form of an enterprise**
(e.g. choice of legal form for tax reasons)

65 **Rechtspersönlichkeit** f.
rechtsfähig
nichtrechtsfähig

= **legal personality**
= **having legal personality**
= **devoid of legal personality**

66 **juristische Person** f.
∼ ∼ **des privaten Rechts**
∼ ∼ **des öffentlichen Rechts**

= **body corporate**
= ∼ ∼ **under private law**
= ∼ ∼ **under public law**
(in Germany)

67 **Verselbständigung** f.
rechtliche ∼
wirtschaftliche ∼
(eines öffentlichen Betriebs)

= **corporate autonomy**
= **legal autonomy**
= **economic autonomy**
(of a public enterprise)

68 **wirtschaftliche Verselbständigung** f.
(eines öffentlichen Betriebs, z.B. durch Annahme der Rechtsform einer GmbH)

= **attainment of operating autonomy**
(of a public enterprise, e.g. by incorporation under company law)

69 **Hoheitsbetrieb** m. = non-autonomous business unit
(z.B. Verwaltungsdruckerei) (within an administration e.g. printing department)

70 **Selbstverwaltung** f. = self-administration; self-government

71 **Finanzautonomie** f. = financial autonomy
finanzielle Selbständigkeit f. = financial independence

72 **öffentliches Recht** n. = public law
(Das öffentliche Recht regelt die Beziehungen des Staates als Hoheitsträger zum Staatsbürger, die Organisation des Staates sowie die Beziehung verschiedener Hoheitsträger untereinander.) (Public law governs the relations of the State as sovereign authority with the citizen; the organization of the State; the relations of various sovereign authorities with each other.)

72a **Verwaltungsrecht** n. ± administrative law
(im deutschen Recht, Gesamtheit der Rechtssätze, die das hoheitliche Tätigwerden der öffentlichen Verwaltung bestimmen;
im englischen Recht, regelt die Organisation, die Pflichten sowie die gerichtlichen und gerichtsähnlichen Befugnisse der vollziehenden Gewalt;
hierzu gehört auch der Bereich des Verfassungsrechts, der die Wahrnehmung von Aufgaben der vollziehenden Gewalt durch solche Personen regelt, die verfassungsrechtlich verantwortlich sind; vom öffentlichen Recht der USA stark beeinflußt) (in German law, the totality of legal provisions which govern the sovereign activity of the public administration;
in English law, the law relating to organization, duties and judicial and quasi-judicial powers of the Executive;

that branch of constitutional law consisting of the rules governing the exercise of executive functions by those persons constitutionally responsible; influenced by example of public law in the USA)

73 **öffentlich-rechtliches Unternehmen** n. ± enterprise established under public law; public corporation

74 **Anstalt** f. **(des öffentlichen Rechts); öffentliche Anstalt** f. = public institution; institution established under public law
(Personen- und Sachgesamtheit, die in der Hand eines Trägers öffentlicher Verwaltung einem öffentlichen Zweck dient; kann rechtsfähig oder nichtrechtsfähig sein; (a combination of human and material resources which is placed in the hands of a public administrative body, to serve an objective of public policy; it may or may not have a legal personality.

in Großbritannien entsprechen viele »nichtministerielle öffentliche Körperschaften« [sogenannte *quangos* – quasi-autonome nichtbehördliche Organisationen] diesem Muster.)

In Great Britain many non-departmental public bodies [so-called quangos – quasi-autonomous non-governmental organizations] fit this pattern.)

75 **Körperschaft f. (des öffentlichen Rechts)**

(in Deutschland: gekennzeichnet durch die Selbstverwaltung ihrer Mitglieder und Beschränkung der öffentlichen Hand auf die Rechtsaufsicht; in Großbritannien: ähnliche Verhältnisse, aber mehr Spielraum für Mitwirkung der Behörden)

± **corporation established under public law; statutory corporation; public corporation**
(in Germany: distinguished by its operational autonomy, with the role of the public authorities restricted to legal supervision; in Great Britain: generally similar, but greater scope for government intervention)

76 **landesunmittelbare Anstalt f.; landesunmittelbare Körperschaft f.**

≠ tp.: *Land* institution; *Land* corporation

77 **bundesunmittelbare Anstalt f.; bundesunmittelbare Körperschaft f.**

≠ tp.: Federal institution; Federal corporation

78 **Liegenschafts- und Mobilienverwaltung f.**
(nutzt als öffentlicher Betrieb öffentliches Vermögen)

± **property board;**
~ **agency**
(part of a public enterprise which manages land and property or movable capital assets e.g. GB: British Rail Property Board, within British Rail)

79 **Gebührenanstalt f.**
(s. Nr. 285)
(Anstalt, deren Ausgaben durch Gebühren ausgeglichen werden)

± **fee-charging institution**
(s. No. 285)
(any public institution whose expenses are met by fees and charges; e.g. in GB: HM Land Registry)

80 **Rechtsbeziehungen fpl.**
(des öffentlichen Betriebs zu Dritten)

= **legal relationship**
(of a public enterprise to third parties)

81 **Eigengesellschaft f.**
(Kapitalgesellschaft, deren gesam-

= **joint-stock company wholly owned by the public sector**
(joint-stock company whose entire

| | tes Kapital einem oder mehreren Gemeinwesen gehört; in Deutschland sehr verbreitet, erscheint aber wenig in GB) | | capital is owned by one and more public authorities; very common in Germany, but seldom found in GB) |

82 **Stiftung** f.
(des öffentlichen und des privaten Rechts)
± **foundation**
(under public law and private law)

83 **öffentliche Einrichtung** f.
Verwaltungseinrichtung f.
(nichtwirtschaftliche Anstalt oder Körperschaft, eingegliedert in eine Gebietskörperschaft [z.B. Schule, Universität]; arbeitet nicht mit dem Ziel der Kostendeckung und hat keine betriebliche Organisation)
± **public institution**
± **administrative entity**
(non-commercial body, part of a territorial authority [e.g. school or polytechnic] which is not required to meet its costs and is not structured for commercial operation)

84 **Finanzmonopol** n.
Staatsmonopol n.
= **financial monopoly**
= **State monopoly**

85 **Monopolverwaltung** f.
(als öffentlicher Betrieb anzusehen; in Deutschland: Branntweinmonopol; Zündwarenmonopol [bis 1982];
in Großbritannien: keine in der jüngsten Zeit)
= **administration of a monopoly**
(seen as public enterprise;
in Germany; brandy monopoly; matches monopoly [till 1982];
in Great Britain: none in modern times)

86 **Handelsrecht** n.
(Oberbegriff)
= **commercial law**
(generic term)

87 **Gesellschaftsrecht** n.
(Unterbegriff)
= **company law**
(part of commercial law)

88 **Haftungsbeschränkung** f.
= **limitation of liability**

89 **Umwandlung** f.
(z.B. eines Eigenbetriebs in eine Aktiengesellschaft)
= **change of corporate form**
(e.g. transformation of a municipal trading fund activity into a public limited company)

90 **Einmanngesellschaft** f.
= **joint-stock company with only one owner**

91 **Gesellschaft** f. (AG, GmbH)
= **public company** (*AG* = public limited company [PLC]; *GmbH* = company with limited liability [Co.Ltd.])

(privatrechtliches Unternehmen, das öffentlich registriert ist – **kann** auch als Einmanngesellschaft öffentliches Eigentum sein)

(company incorporated under private law, but which has a public status and may even be in public ownership e.g. British Nuclear Fuels Ltd.)

92 **Holding** f.;
Konzernspitze f.;
Dachgesellschaft f.;
Konzernmuttergesellschaft f.
(in Deutschland und Großbritannien: Die Holdings von öffentlichen Unternehmen sind größtenteils privatrechtlich organisiert.
In Deutschland braucht z.b. eine Konzernmuttergesellschaft nicht notwendigerweise eine reine Holding-Gesellschaft zu sein, sondern kann eigene Betriebe haben.)

= holding company

(In Germany and Great Britain, the holdings of public enterprises are mainly operated under the provisions of private company law.
In Germany a *Konzernmuttergesellschaft* for example may not only be a holding company but may have enterprises of its own.)

93 staatliche **Holding-Gesellschaft** f.; **öffentlich-rechtliche Holding-Gesellschaft** f.

± State holding company; holding company organized under public law

94 **Konzern** m.
Unterkonzern m.

± industrial group
± division within a group

95 **privatrechtliche Unternehmen** npl. **der öffentlichen Hand**
Kapitalgesellschaft f.
Aktiengesellschaft f. **(AG)**
Gesellschaft f. **mit beschränkter Haftung (GmbH)**

= public sector business established under private law
= joint-stock company
= public limited company (PLC)
= company with limited liability (Co. Ltd.)

96 **betriebswirtschaftliche Grundsätze** mpl.

= principles of operating in a commercial manner

97 **Gemischtwirtschaftsunternehmung** f.

= mixed economy

98 **gemischtwirtschaftliches Unternehmen** n.
(Kapitalgesellschaft, von der die öffentliche Hand mindestens 25% der Anteile besitzt:
in Deutschland: z.B. Volkswagenwerk [VW], Rheinisch-Westfälische Elektrizitäts-AG [REW];
in Großbritannien:

± business with mixed ownership

(joint-stock company of which public authorities own at least 25% of the shares;
in Germany: Volkswagenwerk [VW], Rheinisch-Westfälische Elektrizitäts-AG [RWE];
in Great Britain:

British Petroleum [BP] und National Nuclear Corporation [NNC])

British Petroleum [BP] and National Nuclear Corporation [NNC])

99 **Beteiligungsunternehmen** n.

(Unternehmen, an dem ein anderes beteiligt ist, das einen wesentlichen Einfluß ausübt)

= **undertaking owned by more than one organization**

(company, part of whose share capital is owned by another organization, which is able to wield significant influence)

100 **verbundenes Unternehmen** n.

= **company forming part of an industrial group**

101 **Staatsbeteiligung** fpl.; **Beteiligung** f. **der öffentlichen Hand an einem Unternehmen**

= **State participation**

102 **staatliche Kapitalbeteilung** f.

± **State equity holding**

103 **Beteiligungsbericht** m. (der Bundesregierung)

≠ tp.: Report of the Federal Government on participant State equity holdings

104 **Beteiligungsverwaltung** f.

± **administration of State equity holdings**

105 **Mehrheits-** und **Minderheitsaktienbesitz** m.

= **equity shareholding: majority** and **minority**

106 **Sperrminorität** f.

= **blocking minority shareholding** ("golden share")

107 **Nebenabreden** fpl. (zur Sicherung des beherrschenden Einflusses der öffentlichen Hand)

= **subsidiary agreements** (to safeguard the dominating influence of the public authorities)

108 **beherrschender Einfluß** m. (z.B.: Die öffentliche Hand übt einen beherrschenden Einfluß auf ein gemischtwirtschaftliches Unternehmen aus.)

= **dominating influence** (e.g. where public authorities exercise a dominating influence on an enterprise with mixed public/private sector participation)

109 **beherrschtes Unternehmen** n. (Unternehmen, an dem ein anderes zu mehr als 50% beteiligt ist oder über das ein anderes einen beherrschenden Einfluß ausübt)

= **subsidiary company** (company in which more than 50% of its share capital is owned by another organization, which thereby has a controlling interest)

71

110 ≠ Üv.: Morrisonsche Prinzipien npl.
(Modell der staatlichen Körperschaft, in GB vom ehemaligen Minister Herbert Morrison eingeführt und in der Gesetzgebung der Nachkriegsjahre verankert)

Morrisonian principles
(model of a State corporation, introduced by the former Minister Herbert Morrison and anchored in post-war legislation)

111 **Selbstverwaltungsprinzip** n.
(einer öffentlich-rechtlichen Körperschaft)

± **arm's length principle**

112 **Zweckverband** m.

(*Joint board* and *joint authority* sind Bezeichnungen für einen Zusammenschluß von kommunalen Verwaltungseinheiten zur Wahrnehmung einer oder mehrerer Leistungsaufgaben.
Ein Zweckverband ist ein rechtsfähiger Zusammenschluß von Gemeinden oder Gemeindeverbänden zur gemeinsamen Erfüllung bestimmter Aufgaben.)

± **ad-hoc authority; joint board; joint authority; consortium**
("Joint board" or "joint authority" is used to describe a combination of local authorities for providing a service or services.

The *Zweckverband* is a joint local government body with legal status created to carry out one or more specific tasks.)

112a **Sonderbehörde** f.
(nur für einen bestimmten öffentlichen Aufgabenbereich zuständig)

± **ad-hoc authority**
(only responsible for one single service)

113 **Freiverband** m.
(auf freiwilliger Basis)

± **voluntary association**

114 **Pflichtverband** m.
(durch Beschluß der zuständigen Behörde)

± **compulsory association**
(by order of the relevant public authority)

115 **beliehene Unternehmer** mpl.
(natürliche oder juristische Personen des Privatrechts, die hoheitliche Funktionen im eigenen Namen und meist auch auf eigene Rechnung, aber im Auftrag des Staates ausüben, ohne Teil der Staatsorganisation zu sein;
in Deutschland: z.B. Technischer Überwachungsverein – TÜV; in GB: Britisches Institut für Normung *[BSI]*)

± **contracted undertaker**
(individuals or legal entity organized under private law carrying out sovereign functions on behalf of the State on their own account and without being part of government)

in Germany: Technical Supervision Association *[TÜV]*; in GB: British Standards Institute [BSI])

116 **Betriebsführungsvertrag** m.
(Ein Dritter, z.b. eine Betriebsführungsgesellschaft/Betriebsgesellschaft führt den Betrieb gegen Entgelt auf Rechnung des Gemeinwesens, das das Unternehmensrisiko trägt, z.b. in GB
– Forschungs- und Entwicklungsarbeit in der Verteidigungsindustrie
– Gesellschaft zur Durchführung der Nationalen Gartenschau 1986)

= management contract
(A third party, e.g. a management contractor, carries out a function on behalf of a public agency, with the public purse carrying the commercial risk, e.g. in GB

– research and development work in defence industries

– National Garden Festival 1986 [Stoke-on-Trent, Staffordshire] Ltd.)

117 **öffentlich gebundenes Unternehmen** n.

± **publicly regulated enterprise**
(company regulated by local or central Government)

118 **Regiebetrieb** m.
(Verwaltungsbetrieb; reiner Regiebetrieb)
(s. Nr. 118a, 532;
organisatorisch ausgegliederter Teil der Verwaltung zur Erfüllung besonderer Aufgaben nach betriebswirtschaftlichen Grundsätzen; erscheint im Haushalt des Trägers brutto, d.h. mit allen Ausgaben und Einnahmen, z.B. Fuhrpark, Brennstoffversorgung, Verwaltungsfunktion;
in GB: Bauabteilung)

± **in-house services;**
trading fund activity

(s. No. 118a, 532;
organizationally separate part of an administration to fulfil specific tasks on a business orientated basis; both its gross expenditure and receipts appear in the budget of its owning body, e.g. transport pool, fuel supply, in-house printing department;

in GB: construction and maintenance department)

118a **Bauabteilung** f. **einer Territorialverwaltung**
(In Großbritannien ist die Bezeichnung *direct labour organization* reserviert für die Bauabteilung einer Territorialverwaltung; seit 1980 mit getrennter Kontoführung im Rahmen kommunaler Finanzstruktur.)

± **direct labour organization (DLO)**

(expression normally reserved in GB for the construction and maintenance department of a local authority; since 1980 a DLO has had to be organized as a unit with separately identifiable accounts within the local authority's financial structure.)

119 **Betriebsleiter** m.
(eines Regiebetriebs)
(ist Angehöriger des öffentlichen Dienstes)

= **manager**
(of a direct labour organization)
(is a public service employee)

73

120	Weisungsgebundenheit f. (Bindung des Betriebsleiters eines Regiebetriebs an die Anweisungen der übergeordneten Stelle)	=	duty to comply with instructions (duty of a manager of a trading fund activity to comply with instructions from the superior body)
121	Satzung f.; Betriebssatzung f.	=	articles of association
122	Satzungsrecht n.	=	statutory law
123	Satzungsgewalt f. (Rechtsetzungsbefugnis von Selbstverwaltungskörperschaften)	±	right to issue bye-laws (legislative competence of self-governing bodies)
124	Mustersatzung f.	=	model articles of association
125	Geschäftsordnung f. eine ~ erlassen	= =	standing orders to promulgate ~ ~
126	Mustergeschäftsordnung f. (z.B. Geschäftsordnung der Geschäftsleitung eines Betriebs)	=	model rules of procedure (e.g. the rules of procedure for conducting an enterprise)
127	Geschäftsleitung f.; Betriebsleitung f.	=	management of an enterprise
128	Geschäftsführung f.	=	management (as an activity)
129	Geschäftsführer m.	±	Managing Director; administrative head
130	Werkleitung f.; Geschäftsleitung f. Werkleiter m.; Geschäftsleiter m.	= =	operational management line manager
131	leitender Angestellter m.	=	executive manager
132	Vorstand m. (Direktoren öffentlich-rechtlicher Unternehmen und Anstalten) (in Deutschland: geschäftsführendes Organ von öffentlich-rechtlichen Unternehmen und Aktiengesellschaften, das durch ein weiteres Organ, den Verwaltungsrat bzw. Aufsichtsrat, überwacht wird; in Großbritannien besteht eine Vielzahl ähnlicher Verhältnisse.)	±	executive board (of directors of public companies and public corporations) (in Germany: the executive organ of businesses established under public law and of public limited companies which is itself scrutinized by the supervisory committee; in Great Britain: a variety of broadly similar arrangements exist.)

132a **Vorstand** m. = **executive committee**

133 **Aufsicht** f. = **control; supervision**

134 **Unternehmensleitung** f. = **(Main) Board of Directors**
(in GB Aufsichtsrat einschließlich Vorstand) (including executive directors)

135 **Aufsichtsrat** m. ± **Supervisory Board**
(in Deutschland: das gesetzlich vorgeschriebene Organ in einer Aktiengesellschaft zur Überwachung des Vorstands; in Großbritannien besteht der Aufsichtsrat nicht in einer gesetzlich vorgeschriebenen Form; bei einer Aktiengesellschaft setzt er sich aus geschäftsführenden und nichthauptamtlichen Direktoren zusammen.) (in Germany: legally prescribed body in a public limited company which supervises the Executive Board of Management; in Great Britain the legal form of the Supervisory Board does not exist. The board of a PLC includes both executive and non-executive directors.)

136 **Hauptversammlung** f. = **Annual General Meeting (AGM)**
(Beschlußorgan der Gesellschafter [Aktionäre] einer Aktiengesellschaft) (decision-making body of shareholders in a public limited company)

137 ≠ **Executive Board Member**
Üv.: geschäftsführendes Vorstandsmitglied n.
(in GB: Vorstandsmitglied mit geschäftsführenden Aufgaben in einem Unternehmen) (in GB: Member of a Board of Directors who has executive functions within the enterprise)

138 ≠ **Non-Executive Board Member**
Üv.: nichthauptamtliches Vorstandsmitglied n.
(besteht nicht im deutschen Gesellschaftsrecht; in GB: Vorstandsmitglied, das einen Beitrag zur allgemeinen Richtung eines Betriebs leistet, aber keine geschäftsführenden Aufgaben besitzt) (in GB: Member of a Board of Directors who contributes to general policy but carries no executive functions)

139 **Überwachung** f. der Geschäftsleitung = **supervision of the management**
(durch den Aufsichtsrat/Verwaltungsrat) (by the Supervisory Board)

140 **Werkausschuß** m.
(des Eigenbetriebs)
(entscheidet über wichtige Angelegenheiten des Eigenbetriebs und übt die ständige Kontrolle über die Werkleitung aus)

± policy-setting committee
(for a municipal undertaking)
(committee which takes policy decisions on the operation of an autonomous municipal enterprise and controls the operational management)

141 **Gemeindevertreter** m. **im Werksausschuß**

= elected member of a local authority, in the policy committee

142 **Arbeitnehmervertreter** m. **im Werksausschuß**

= representative of the work force, in the policy committee

143 **Verwaltungsrat** m.
(in Deutschland:
Aufsichtsorgan gegenüber dem Vorstand in öffentlich-rechtlichen Unternehmen; bis zu einem gewissen Grade dem Aufsichtsrat der Aktiengesellschaft vergleichbar;
in Großbritannien:
ähnliche Organe in öffentlichen Unternehmen [und Aktiengesellschaften], wobei der Vorstand zum Teil stimmberechtigter Teil des Verwaltungsrats ist; [z.B. *main boards* in nationalisierten Unternehmen und »Spezialausschüsse« in Kommunalbehörden])

± policy-setting committee
(for a public enterprise)
(in Germany:
body which supervises management in enterprises established under public law; to a certain extent comparable with supervisory board of a public limited company;

in Great Britain:
broadly similar arrangements in the public sector where managers may sometimes be represented [for example, "main boards" of nationalized industries, and special-purpose committees of local authorities])

144 **Steuerungsausschuß** m.; **Ad-hoc-Ausschuß** m.
(Ausschuß zur Kontrolle spezifischer, meist zeitbegrenzter Funktionen)

± steering committee
(senior management committee, for high-level supervision of a specific, usually time-limited, function)

145 **Träger** m.; **Trägerschaft** f.; **Trägerkörperschaft** f.
(Eigentümer eines öffentlichen Betriebs oder öffentlichen Unternehmens)

= body ultimately responsible for a public enterprise
(owner of a public enterprise or public undertaking)

146 **Trägerverband** m.
(bestehend aus mehreren Trägern; in GB: z.B. Zweckverband von territorialen Behörden zum Betrieb

= association of bodies ultimately responsible for a public enterprise
(in GB: e.g. joint board of local authorities [to operate an airport];

	eines Flughafens; in Deutschland: auch bei einem Träger)		in Germany: such an association can consist of a single body)
147	**Behörde** f.	±	public authority
148	**vorgesetzte Behörde** f.	=	superior authority
149	**Aufsichtsbehörde** f.	=	supervisory authority
	Einwirkung f. **der** ~ (durch Beanstandung, Weisung oder Selbsteintritt)	=	intervention of the ~ ~ (through complaints, directive or own initiative)
	Aufsichtsrecht npl. **(der Aufsichtsbehörde)**	=	rights of supervision
	Beanstandungsrecht n.;	=	right to raise objection
	Weisungsrecht n.	=	~ to issue directives
	Selbsteintrittsrecht n.	=	~ to action on own initiative
150	**aufsichtsführender Minister** m.	=	the responsible (sponsoring) Minister
151	≠ Üv.: Erster parlamentarischer Staatssekretär m. des Finanzministeriums (in Großbritannien: Minister [nicht Beamter], dem *Chancellor of the Exchequer* [Finanzminister] untergeordnet; ist Kabinettsmitglied)	=	Chief Secretary to the Treasury (in Great Britain: Cabinet-level Treasury minister responsible for public expenditure)
152	≠ Üv.: Arbeitsgruppe f. im Finanzministerium zur Kontrolle öffentlicher Unternehmen		public enterprises group in the Treasury
153	≠ Üv.: öffentliche Ausgaben-Planung f. (interministerielle Verhandlungen über Umfang öffentlicher Aufgaben)		public expenditure surveys (inter-departmental negotiations within central Government to determine the size and scope of public expenditure)
154	≠ Üv.: Parlamentarischer Ausschuß m. für öffentliche Rechnungslegung		**Public Accounts Committee (PAC)**

155	(ministerielle) Fachaufsicht f. (von einer staatlichen Fachbehörde ausgeübte Aufsicht; umfaßt sowohl die Kontrolle der Rechtmäßigkeit als auch der Zweckmäßigkeit einer übertragenen Aufgabe)	±	ministerial control (form of supervisory control both as to the legality and the expediency of delegated functions)
156	ministerielle Verfügung f.	=	ministerial order; ~ determination
157	Enteignungsvollmacht f.	=	power of compulsory purchase
158	Gesetzentwurf m. (in Großbritannien: Die öffentliche Hand und öffentliche Unternehmen können um Vollmachten ersuchen entweder durch *public bills* [Gesetze mit allgemeiner Gültigkeit] oder durch *private bills* [Gesetze zur Erteilung von Vollmachten an öffentliche Unternehmen])	=	Bill (public authorities and public enterprises can seek powers either through public bills or private bills)
159	gesetzlich, auf dem Verordnungswege festgelegte Vollmachten fpl.	=	Statutory Powers and Instruments
160	Üv.: Kreditplafond m. für Sektoren der öffentlichen Wirtschaft	≠	Borrowing Powers Act (sets upper limits, by Parliamentary authority, to borrowing by public sector agencies)
161	Sonderausschüsse mpl. des Parlaments	±	select committees, of Parliament
162	parlamentarische Kontrolle f. (gegenüber der Regierung)	=	parliamentary control
163	gerichtliche Überprüfung f.	=	judicial review
164	verwaltungsmäßige Überprüfung f.	=	administrative review
165	gesetzlich vorgeschriebene Enquete f.	=	Public Enquiries
166	parastaatliche gemeinnützige Einrichtung f. (Anstalt)	±	non-departmental public body; QUANGO (quasi-autonomous non-governmental organization)

167	Bundeskartellamt n.	±	Monopolies and Mergers Commission

168 Rundfunkanstalt f.
(z.B. *British Broadcasting Corporation* [*BBC*]; in Deutschland auf Länderbasis organisiert)

± broadcasting authority
(e.g. British Broadcasting Corporation [BBC]; in Germany: organized on a *Laender* basis)

169 Verbraucherbeirat m.   ± Consumer Council

170   ≠   Crown Agents
Üv.: Königliche Spezialagentur f.
(Bank und Handelsgesellschaft zur Verfügung fremder Regierungen für Finanz-, Handels- und Grundstücksgeschäfte)

(UK Government agency which acts on behalf of foreign governments in financial, trading and real estate matters)

171 Beamter m.
(In Deutschland sind Beschäftigte in öffentlichen Betrieben oft Beamte.)

± public official; civil servant
(Many of the employees of public enterprises in Germany are permanent public officials or civil servants.)

172   ≠   Crown Servants
Üv.: Oberbegriff für Beamte mpl. und Militärpersonal n.
(In einigen Fällen kann ein öffentliches Unternehmen »im Dienste der Krone« [*Crown Servant*] stehen, z.B. Königliche Waffenfabriken [*ROFs*].)

(In some cases, an enterprise can be a Crown Servant, for example, Royal Ordnance Factories.)

173 Behördenleiter m.; leitender Beamter m. einer Behörde   = chief executive of a public body

174 Intendant m.
(in Deutschland:
auf Leiter von Rundfunkanstalten und kulturellen Einrichtungen beschränkt)

± Director-General
(in Germany:
the term *Intendant* is restricted mainly to the head of broadcasting and cultural organizations)

175 Gemeindeordnung f.
(in Deutschland:
Landesgesetz für die Gemeinden des Landes;
in Großbritannien:
parlamentarisch angenommene Gesetze)

± Local Government Act
(in Germany:
Land legislation governing the municipalities;
in Great Britain:
national legislation)

176	soziale Marktwirtschaft f. (in Deutschland: politische Bezeichnung für die Wirtschaftsform der Bundesrepublik Deutschland – entstanden nach der Währungsreform 1948, gekennzeichnet durch den Versuch einer Kombination von Wettbewerb und Wohlfahrtsstaat)	±	social market economy (in Germany: political description for the economic system established in the Federal Republic of Germany after the currency reform of 1948 and characterized by a combination of competition and welfare State)
177	Opportunitätskosten pl. (wirtschaftswissenschaftlicher Begriff zur Bezeichnung verpaßter Alternativen)	=	opportunity costs (economic term for forgone alternatives)
178	soziale Opportunitätskosten pl. (verpaßte Alternative unter Einschluß gesamtgesellschaftlicher Kosten z.B. Kosten der Umweltverschmutzung)	=	social opportunity costs (forgone alternative when all costs arising are included, e.g. cost of pollution)
179	wirtschaftliche Rettungsaktion f. (z.B. Rettung von Großkonzernen durch Verstaatlichung)	=	economic salvage operation (e.g. the rescue of major companies by taking them into public ownership)
180	Stabilitätspolitik f. (In der Bundesrepublik wurde der Begriff ursprünglich auch als Vollbeschäftigungspolitik verstanden, wird aber neuerdings mehr mit einer Politik der Preisstabilisierung gleichgesetzt.)	±	anti-inflation policy (In Germany stabilization policy originally described measures designed to maintain a high level of employment. It is now almost synonymous, however, with anti-inflation politics.)

6.2 Begriffe in der Gesetzgebung über Erstellung oder Kontrolle von öffentlichen Betrieben

Terms used in legislation and regulations establishing or controlling public enterprises

181	Entschädigung f. für Nationalisierung	=	compensation for nationalization of assets
182	Kapitalausstattung f.	=	capital debt

183 **Kapitalerstausstattung** f. (zinstragend)
(in Form einer Verbindlichkeit gegenüber dem zuständigen Ministerium, die von diesem mit Zustimmung des Finanzministers festgelegt wird)

± **commencing capital debt**
(bearing interest)
(a debt due to the Minister on vesting day of an amount determined by him with Treasury approval)

184 **vorbereitender Ausschuß** m. **für Nationalisierung**

= **organizing committee for a nationalized industry**

185 **Fachaufsichtsbehörde** f.
(Fachaufsichtsministerium)
(s. Nr. 155)

= **supervising department**
(s. No. 155)

186 **Kriterien** npl. **für die Berufung von Vorstandsmitgliedern**
(In Großbritannien:
»Der Vorstandsvorsitzende, sein Stellvertreter und andere Vorstandsmitglieder sind einem Kreis von Personen zu entnehmen, die nach Ansicht des Ministers große Erfahrungen im Verkehr in allen Sparten haben sowie in kommerzieller und finanzieller Hinsicht, in Verwaltungsfragen, Arbeitnehmerorganisation oder Vertretung von Verbraucherinteressen.« § 1 [4] des Flughafenbehördengesetzes von 1965;
in Deutschland sind die Bestimmungen für Körperschaften öffentlichen Rechts jeweils in deren Satzung bzw. Gründungsakte (z.B. Bundesbankgesetz) geregelt; für die meisten öffentlichen Unternehmen (als AG oder GmbH) gelten die gesellschaftsrechtlichen Regelungen wie für private Unternehmen.)

= **criteria of appointing boards**
(in Great Britain:
"The chairman, deputy chairman and other members of the Authority shall be appointed from among persons who appear to the Minister to have had wide experience of transport, all forms of transport industry, commercial or financial matters, administration, the organization of workers, or the representation of the interests of consumers." Section 1 [4] Airport Authorities Act 1965;

in Germany the criteria of appointing boards are regulated in the by-laws or statutes of public corporations (for example German Federal Bank Act); company law regulations applying to private enterprises also apply to most of the public undertakings [as *AG* or *GmbH*].)

187 **Gründungsdatum** n. **eines Unternehmens; Gründungstag** m.
(in gesetzlicher Form festgelegtes Datum, zu dem ein öffentliches Unternehmen begründet wird oder Grundstücke bzw. andere Vermögenswerte übernimmt)

= **vesting date; time of vesting; appointed day of an undertaking**
(date specified in an Act on which a public enterprise comes into being or takes possession of land or property)

188	**Rechte** npl. **und Pflichten** fpl. (öffentlicher Körperschaften) (Beispiel aus dem britischen Luftfahrtkörperschaftsgesetz von 1967, § 3 [2]; »... die Körperschaften sollen das Recht haben..., alles zu tun, was darauf abgestellt ist, die Wahrnehmung ihrer Aufgaben zu fördern... bzw. die anderen Funktionen, die der Körperschaft übertragen oder zugewiesen wurden von oder nach diesem Gesetz, oder das, was dazu führen kann, daß solche Funktionen wahrgenommen werden."«)	=	**powers and duties** (of public corporations) (an example of general wording [Section 3 [2] Air Corporations Act 1967: "... the corporations shall have power... to do anything which is calculated to facilitate the discharge of their functions... or of any other functions conferred or imposed on the corporation by or under this Act, or is incident or conducive to the discharge of any such functions".)
189	**Recht** n. **zur Kreditaufnahme** (Vollmacht zur Aufnahme von Krediten auch als Kontokredit [bis zu Grenzen, die in diesem Gesetz festgelegt wurden], falls benötigt zur Abdeckung von Verbindlichkeiten und zur Wahrnehmung von Funktionen)	=	**borrowing powers** (powers to raise loans or overdrafts [to limits set out in the Act] if needed to meet obligations and discharge functions)
190	**Vollmacht** f. **zur Informationseinholung** (Vollmacht für Minister zur Anforderung von Informationen bei öffentlichen Unternehmen)	=	**power of Ministers** to require information from public enterprises
191	Üv.: Vollmacht f. für Minister zur Erteilung von Anweisungen an nationalisierte Unternehmen	≠	**power of Ministers to issue directions to nationalized industries**
192	**Konzept** n. **der allgemeinen ministeriellen Richtlinienkompetenz** (Zielvorgabe)	=	**concept of general direction as given by Ministers** (target setting)
193	**Richtlinienkompetenz** f. (in Deutschland Vollmacht [des Bundeskanzlers], die Richtlinien der Regierungspolitik zu erlassen; Ausübung der Vollmacht zur Herausgabe allgemeiner Anweisungen z.B. des Trägers gegenüber dem öffentlichen Unternehmen;	=	**power to issue general directions** (in Germany, authority [of the head of government] to decide on government policy; power e.g. of the authority responsible for the public enterprise to decide on the policy to be pursued;

in Großbritannien Vollmacht für Minister zur Herausgabe von allgemeinen Anweisungen; [§ 4 *Air Corporations Act* 1967]: »Der Minister kann, nach Beratung mit... der Körperschaft, Anweisungen von allgemeinem Charakter erteilen bezüglich der Art und Weise, in der die Körperschaft ihre Funktionen ausübt und wahrnimmt, in Bezug auf Angelegenheiten, die nach Ansicht des Ministers die nationalen Interessen berühren dürften; und... die Körperschaft... soll sämtlichen Anweisungen Folge leisten."

in Great Britain, Minister's power to issue general directions [Section 4 Air Corporations Act 1967]: "The Minister may, after consultation with ... the corporation, give directions of a general character as to the exercise and performance by the corporation of its functions in relation to matters appearing [to the Minister] to affect the national interests; and the corporation ... shall give effect to any directions.")

194 **Kompetenz f. zum Erlaß spezifischer Richtlinien**
(Nach dem Verkehrsgesetz von 1972, § 37 [4], kann der Minister den Vorstand anweisen, daß er einen Teil seiner Unternehmung aufgibt, irgendwelche Vermögenswerte der Unternehmung veräußert, Guthaben einzieht oder jedwede Vollmacht, die er hat, ausübt, um dem Unternehmen gegebene Garantien rückgängig zu machen.
In Deutschland ist diese Kompetenz generell nicht gegeben; in Sonderfällen (z.B. im Energiewirtschaftsgesetz vom 19. 12. 1977, etwa in den §§ 12 ff.) wird die Verordnungs-Ermächtigung spezifisch erteilt.)

± **power of specific direction**
(Under Transport Act 1972 Section 37 [4], the Minister could direct the [British Railways] Board to discontinue any of their undertaking, dispose of any assets held by them, call in any loans made by them or exercise any power they may possess to revoke any guarantees given by them.

In Germany this power is not generally given; in specific cases such as the German Energy Act of 19 December 1977, Art. 12 et seq., the power of specific direction is expressly granted.)

195 **Rechtsverordnung f.**

(Nach Art. 80 GG können die Bundesregierung, ein Bundesminister oder die Landesregierungen durch Gesetz ermächtigt werden, Rechtsverordnungen zu erlassen. Dabei müssen Inhalt, Zweck und Ausmaß der erteilten Ermächtigung im Gesetz bestimmt werden.)

≠
tp.: statutory order
(According to art. 80 of the Basic Law, the Federal Government, a Federal Minister or the *Land* governments may be authorized by a law to issue ordinances. The content, purpose and scope of the authorization so conferred must be set forth in this law.)

196 ≠
Üv.: Rechtsverordnung f.

(Der Begriff »Rechtsverordnung« ist ein umfassender Ausdruck, der alle – dem *Statutory Instruments Act* 1946 unterworfenen – Formen der untergeordneten Gesetzgebung kennzeichnet.

Mit zahlreichen parlamentarischen Gesetzen erhalten die Minister die Vollmacht, detaillierte Anweisungen oder Regeln für öffentliche Unternehmen zu erlassen. Gesetzesvorlagen müssen normalerweise »dem Parlament unterbreitet« werden und können dem Verfahren der »negativen Entschließung« [treten in Kraft, sofern keine Einwendungen erhoben werden], oder dem der »positiven Entschließung« [erfordert einen Beschluß des Unterhauses] unterworfen sein.)

Statutory Instrument; secondary legislation; Regulations

(The phrase "statutory instrument" is a comprehensive expression which describes all forms of subordinate legislation subject to the Statutory Instruments Act 1946.

Many Acts of Parliament empower Ministers to issue detailed instructions or rules to public enterprises. Statutory Instruments must normally be "laid before Parliament" and can be subject to the "negative resolution" procedure [come into force unless prayed against] or the "positive resolution" procedure [requires a vote on the floor of the House of Commons].)

197 **Leistungskriterium** n.
(in Großbritannien:
Der Minister soll von Zeit zu Zeit einen Reinertrag bezogen auf den Nettovermögenswert festlegen, von dem der Minister annimmt, daß davon Einordnung in dem betreffenden Zeitraum angemessen wäre.

Er kann stattdessen auch eine finanzielle Verpflichtung festlegen, die anders zum Ausdruck kommt als unter Bezugnahme auf den Reinertrag bezogen auf den Nettovermögenswert.

In Deutschland gibt es den Begriff des »Leistungskriteriums« nur im betriebswirtschaftlichen Sinn. Hier wird er vielfach mit der Ertragslage der Unternehmung und ihrer Produktivitätssituation gleichgesetzt.)

± **performance criterion**
(in Great Britain:
The Minister shall from time to time determine a rate of return on net assets which the Minister considers it is reasonable for the corporation to achieve in that period.

He may also substitute for this duty a financial duty expressed otherwise than by reference to a "rate of return on net assets" [Air Corporation Act 1967].

In Germany the concept of "performance criterion" only exists in business administration; here it is often equated with the earning situation of the enterprise and its productivity.)

198	Ermessenskontrolle f.	=	performance control
199	ministerielle Genehmigung f. (erforderlich für bestimmte Handlungen öffentlicher Unternehmen)	=	consent of the Minister (required for certain actions by public enterprises)
200	Genehmigungsvorbehalt m.	=	qualified consent (consent in which certain matters are reserved)
201	zustimmungsbedürftige Geschäfte npl.	=	transactions which require approval
202	Rechnungswesen n. (Es wird üblicherweise verlangt, daß die Rechnungslegung öffentlicher Unternehmen »in einer Form erfolgt, die den besten geschäftlichen Normen entspricht«. Rechnungsprüfer werden normalerweise von der Unternehmung benannt, wobei manchmal die Zustimmung des Ministers erforderlich ist.)	=	accounts (Accounts of public enterprises are usually required to be prepared "in a form which shall conform to the best commercial standards". Auditors are normally appointed by the enterprise, sometimes with the consent of the Minister necessary.)
203	Eigenwirtschaftlichkeit f. (in Deutschland: Verpflichtung zur Deckung des Aufwands durch den Ertrag; in Großbritannien: Die Unternehmung soll ihre Geschäfte so wahrnehmen, daß die Leistung mindestens dafür ausreicht, um die Belastungen zu decken, die normalerweise aus dem Ertrag zu decken sind, [über mehrere Jahre hinweg]. § 3 [1] Zivilluftfahrtsgesetz 1965)	=	obligation to balance (revenue) accounts; ~ ~ break even (in Germany: Expenditure must be met by revenue; in Great Britain: The Authority shall so conduct its business as to secure that its revenue is not less than sufficient for making provision for the meeting of charges properly chargeable to revenue, taking one year with another. Section 3 [1] Civil Aviation Act 1965)
204	Konzessionsträger m. in der öffentlichen Versorgungswirtschaft (In Großbritannien wird der Begriff *statutory undertaker* in einer Reihe von Gesetzen definiert; die Funktionen von *statutory undertakers* sind auf die öffentlichen Un-	=	statutory undertaker (in Great Britain: defined in a number of Acts; and the functions of statutory undertakers have been redistributed among public enterprises by other Acts; Section 63 of Civil Aviation Act

ternehmen erstreckt worden. In § 63 des britischen Zivilluftfahrtsgesetzes von 1949 wird der Begriff »gesetzlich anerkannte Unternehmen« auf jede Person [einschließlich einer Kommunalbehörde] angewandt, die gesetzlich zugelassen ist, um
a) eine Eisenbahn, Kleinbahn, Straßenbahn, ein Straßenverkehrs-, Wasserverkehrs-, Kanal- oder Binnenschiffahrtsunternehmen, einen Hafenbetrieb, Hafen-, Pier- oder Leuchtturmanlagen, oder
b) ein Unternehmen zur Versorgung mit Strom, Gas oder Wasserkraft, oder
c) ein Unternehmen der Wasserversorgung zu erbauen, zu verwalten oder zu betreiben.

Nach dem Gesetz von 1965 wurde die britische Flughafenbehörde [BAA] zur gesetzlich anerkannten Unternehmung erklärt; die Flughafenanlagen wurden damit ein gesetzlich anerkanntes Unternehmen.

in Deutschland:
Übertragung eines Nutzungsrechts an einer öffentlichen Sache zur langfristigen oder dauernden Inanspruchnahme [Verlegung von Schienen, Rohren und Kabeln, Ableitung und Nutzung von Gewässern, Durchführung von Linienverkehr auf öffentlichen Wegen, Nutzung von Hafen- oder Flughafenanlagen u.ä.])

1949 used the definition: »'statutory undertaker' means any person [including a local authority] authorized by any Act to construct work or carry on

a) any railway, light railway, tramway, road transport, water transport, canal, inland navigation, dock, harbour, pier or lighthouse undertaking; or

b) any undertaking for the supply of electricity, gas or hydraulic power; or

c) any undertaking for the supply of water.«

The 1965 Act made the British Airports Authority [BAA] a statutory undertaker, thus putting airport facilities into the class of activities forming a statutory undertaking.

in Germany:
transfer of the right to use public property on a long-term or permanent basis [relocation of railway, pipes or cables, derivation and use of waters, implementation of scheduled services on public roads, use of port and airport facilities etc.])

6.3 Kosten, Finanzierung, Besteuerung und Vergabewesen in öffentlichen Unternehmen

Costs, finance, taxation and procurement in public enterprises

205 öffentliches Kredit- und Versicherungswesen n.

± public banking and insurance

206	Finanzinstitute npl. der öffentlichen Hand	=	public sector financial institutions
207	öffentlich-rechtliches Kreditinstitut n.	≠	tp.: bank incorporated under public law
208	**Sparkassen** fpl.	=	**savings banks**
209	öffentlich-rechtliche Bausparkasse f.	≠	tp.: building societies incorporated under public law
210	**staatliche Kredite** mpl.	=	**Government advances; Exchequer advances**

(In Deutschland erfolgt Kreditgewährung seitens der öffentlichen Hand an Unternehmen nach privatrechtlicher Regelung; daneben können die öffentlichen Unternehmen in der Regel Kredite auf dem Kapitalmarkt in Anspruch nehmen. In Großbritannien erfolgt die Kreditaufnahme dieser Unternehmen in der Regel beim Finanzministerium *[Treasury]*, das sich seinerseits die Mittel auf dem Kapitalmarkt beschaffen kann. Direkte Kreditaufnahme öffentlicher Unternehmen auf dem Kapitalmarkt wird nur als Ausnahme zugelassen, und dann erfolgt sie meist im Ausland. Der Ausdruck »staatliche Kredite« ist in Großbritannien im Nationalen Kreditgesetz 1968 an die Stelle des Ausdrucks »Kredite des Finanzministeriums« getreten.)

(In Germany enterprises are granted credit by public authorities under the provisions of private law; in general public enterprises may also raise loans on the capital market.

In Great Britain public enterprises usually obtain advances from the Treasury which in turn can raise funds from the capital market. Direct borrowings by public undertakings are only admitted as an exception, and such funds are usually raised abroad.

In the National Loans Act 1968, the term "Exchequer advances" was substituted by that of "Government advances" which has been used in Great Britain since that time.)

211 **Bürgschaften** fpl. **des Finanzministeriums** = **Treasury guarantees**

(für Kreditaufnahme öffentlicher Unternehmen bei nichtstaatlichen Stellen; in Großbritannien erfolgt eventuelle Bürgschaftsleistung durch den *Consolidated Fund*. In Deutschland ist die Bürgschaftsgewährung jeweils in den Haushaltsordnungen des Bundes, der Länder und Gemeinden geregelt.)

(on loans raised by some public enterprises from non-Government sources; if called upon, are paid from the Consolidated Fund;

in Germany guarantees on loans are given in accordance with the budget regulations of the Federation, the *Laender* and the communities.)

212 ≠ Üv.: Kreditfonds m. des Finanzministeriums bei der Zentralbank (nach dem *National Loans Act 1968;*

in dieser Form in Deutschland nicht existent; allenfalls vergleichbar mit Kassenkrediten der Bundesbank)

National Loans Fund

(account held by the Treasury at the Bank of England, National Loans Act 1968; in this form, non existent in Germany, might be compared to cash advances extended by the *Bundesbank*)

213 **Sondervermögen** n.
(durch Gesetz abgesonderte und zur Erfüllung bestimmter Aufgaben vorgesehene Vermögensbestandteile einer Gebietskörperschaft;
in Deutschland:
a) die Eigenbetriebe der Gemeinden,
b) Deutsche Bundesbahn,
c) Deutsche Bundespost,
d) ERP-Sondervermögen,

e) Lastenausgleichsfonds;
in Großbritannien:
a) Kommunale Regiebetriebe,
b) Britische Bahnen,
c) Nationaler Kulturhistorischer Fonds,
d) Schottische Entwicklungsagentur)

± **specially designated fund**
(proportion of the assets of a territorial authority, e.g. central or local government, established to carry out specific tasks, e.g.

in Germany:
a) autonomous municipal undertakings,
b) German Federal Railways,
c) German Federal Post Office,
d) European Recovery Program Special Fund,
e) Equalization of War Burdens Fund;
in Great Britain:
a) municipal trading fund activities
b) British Rail,
c) National Heritage Fund,

d) Scottish Development Agency)

214 **mündelsichere Wertpapiere** npl.
(öffentlicher Unternehmen)
(Bestände von Wertpapieren mit staatlicher Bürgschaft erworben von Nachlaßverwaltern, Pensionsfonds usw.; Rechtsgrundlage in GB ist der *Trustee Investment Act* 1961; umfaßt praktisch alle Bürgschaften, die einen regierungsgewährleisteten Zinssatz tragen.
In Deutschland ist der Begriff der mündelsicheren Wertpapiere ein Begriff der Rechtspraxis, der speziell für Versicherungen und deren Anlagen satzungsmäßig geregelt ist.)

= **Trustee Investments**

(Investment by trustees in fixed-interest securities issued in the UK by any public authority or nationalized industry or undertaking in the UK is authorized by the Trustee Investment Act 1961; in effect, covers any securities the payment of interest on which is guaranteed by HM Government.
In Germany trustee investments are a concept of legal practice specified in the bye-laws of insurance companies and their investments.)

215	Üv.: Nationale Girozentrale f.	National Giro Bank
216	**Gewährsträger** m. (Die Gemeinde haftet als Gewährsträger für die Verbindlichkeiten der kommunalen Sparkasse.)	≠ tp.: guarantor (In Germany a local authority guarantees the liability of a municipal savings bank.)
217	**Kapitalmarkt** m. **Geldmarkt** m.	= capital market = money market
218	**Darlehensaufnahme** f.	= raising a loan
219	**Mittelbeschaffung** f. **Mittelverwendung** f. (in beiden Fällen für Investitionen)	= raising of funds; ~ ~ resources = application of resources (in both cases for investment purposes)
220	**Kreditaufnahme** f.	= borrowings
221	**Finanzierungsgesellschaft** f. (in Deutschland: Ermöglichung der Inanspruchnahme von Kapitalmarktmitteln außerhalb des Haushalts des Trägers; auch **Seitenfinanzierung** genannt)	≠ tp.: company formed to raise capital (in Germany: to enable a public enterprise to tap capital reserves other than through the budget of its owning authority; also known in Germany as **"lateral financing"**)
222	**Hauptsumme** f.; **Kapitalhauptsumme** f.	= principal sum
223	**Innenfinanzierung** f.	= internal finance
224	**Eigenfinanzierung** f.; **Selbstfinanzierung** f. (d.h. Finanzierung von Neuinvestitionen aus beibehaltenen Gewinnen)	= self-financing (i.e. financing new investment from retained profits)
225	**Außenfinanzierung** f.	= raising of external capital
226	**Betriebsmittel** npl. **liquide Mittel** npl.	= working capital = cash balances
227	**Umlaufvermögen** n.	= circulating capital

228	Betriebsvermögen n.	=	working capital
229	Betriebsverpachtung f. (Verpachtung des Betriebsvermögens)	=	leasing of working capital
230	Erhaltung f. des Vermögens	=	maintenance of working capital
231	Investition f.	=	investment
	Ersatzinvestition f.	=	replacement investment
	Erweiterungsinvestition f.	=	investment which increases capacity
	Rationalisierungsinvestition f.	=	investment which rationalizes production methods
	Vorratsinvestition f.	=	investment in stocks (inventories)
	Veränderung f. des Lagerbestands	=	changes in stocks (inventories)
232	Anlagevermögen n.	=	fixed capital; ∼ assets
	Anlageänderung f.	=	changes in fixed capital (assets)
	Anlagennachweis m.	=	statement of capital position
233	Finanzanlagen fpl.	=	financial assets
234	Sachanlagen fpl.	=	physical assets
235	Wertminderung f.	=	reduction in value
	Werterhöhung f.	=	increase in value
236	Veräußerung f. von Vermögenswerten	=	sales of assets
237	öffentliche Kreditaufnahme f.	=	Public Sector Borrowing Requirement (PSBR)
238	Kapitalbedarf f.	=	capital requirements; financial requirements
	Kapitalerhöhung f.	=	capital appreciation; increase in capital
	Kapitalherabsetzung f.	=	reduction in capital; writing off
239	Kapitalzuführung f.	=	increase in capital
	Kapitalausstattung f.	=	capitalization
	Kapitalstock m.	=	capital fund
240	Kapitalbeschaffung f.	=	raising capital
	∼ auf dem Kapitalmarkt	=	∼ ∼ in the market

241	**Kapitaldienst** m.	=	servicing capital; interest payments;
	Schuldendienst m. (Verzinsung und Tilgung)	=	debt servicing (interest payments and amortization)
242	**Anschaffungswertprinzip** n.	=	principle of capital replacement
243	**Abschreibung** f.	=	depreciation
	~, **verbrauchsbedingte** (**nutzungsbedingte, technische**)	=	~ through technical obsolescence
	~, **wirtschaftlich bedingte**	=	~ through market obsolescence
	~, **planmäßige**	=	~, anticipated
	~, **außerplanmäßige**	=	~, unanticipated
	~ **auf Wiederbeschaffungskosten**	=	~, at replacement cost
	~ **auf Anschaffungskosten**	=	~ at historic cost
	~, **steuerliche**		capital allowance against tax
	~ **auf öffentliche Anlagen**		amortization of public sector assets
244	**Abschreibungsmethoden** fpl. (z.B. lineare ~, degressive ~, progressive ~, variable ~)	=	methods of depreciation (e.g. straight-line ~ ~ ~ declining-balance ~ ~ ~, progressive ~ ~ ~, variable ~ ~ ~)
245	**Sonderabschreibung** fpl.	=	special provision for depreciation
246	**Zuweisungen** fpl. **zum:** **Abschreibungsfonds** **Erneuerungsfonds** **zu: Rückstellungen** (zur Deckung des Risikos einer Entwertung der Vermögensgüter)	= =	provision for depreciation; sinking fund asset renewal fund (to allow for renewal of capital assets)
247	**Substanzerhaltung** f.	=	maintaining the real value of capital assets
248	**Rückstellung** f. **für Geldentwertung** (z.B. für den Ersatz von Anlagegütern)	±	provision for inflation (to renew capital assets)
249	**Restbuchwert** m., **nutzungsgerecht abgeschriebener; Zeitwert** m.	=	written-down value, reflecting physical use
250	**Tilgungsplan** m.	=	reduction schedule; amortization schedule

251 **Annuität** f.
(jährlich gleichbleibende Schuldendienstleistung, die einen progressiven Tilgungsanteil und einen degressiven Zinsanteil enthält)
= **annuity**
(constant annual debt servicing payment, which involves increasing repayment of capital and decreasing interest payments)

252 **Verlustabschreibung** f.
= **writing off capital**

253 **Löschung** f. **der Kapitalerstausstattungskredite**
(bzw. anderer Kredite seitens der zuständigen Ministerien)
= **writing off (extinguishment of capital debt)**
(by the sponsoring Ministry)

254 **Entschuldung** f.
= **capital reconstruction**

255 **Verlustabschreibung** f. **auf öffentliches Eigenkapital**
(Sonderabschreibung)
= **capital restructuring**
(writing off public dividend capital)

256 **Übernahme** f. **eines Unternehmens durch das Management**
(und teilweise die Belegschaft)
(Bildung einer Quasi-de-Fakto-Produktivgenossenschaft in gesellschaftlicher Form)
= **management buy-out**

(formation of a kind of producer cooperative within the framework of company law)

257 **Etatbindung** f. **des Regiebetriebs**
(Bruttoveranschlagung aller Einnahmen und Ausgaben des Regiebetriebs im Haushaltsplan der Trägerkörperschaft)
= **budget appropriation for a trading fund activity**
(gross budget estimates of expenditures and receipts of a trading fund activity within the budget of its owning body)

258 **Finanzbeziehungen** fpl. **zur Trägerkörperschaft**
= **financial relationships with the ultimate owning body**

259 **Abgrenzung** f.
(z.B. des Betriebsvermögens von dem übrigen Vermögen der Trägerkörperschaft)
= **demarcation**
(e.g. of the working capital of an enterprise from the other assets of its owning body)

260 **Stammkapital** n.; **Grundkapital** n.
(in Deutschland:
bei GmbHs, Eigenbetrieben und öffentlich-rechtlichen Unternehmen;

in GB: allgemeiner Begriff)
= **equity capital**

(in Germany:
applies to private limited companies, wholly owned subsidiaries in the public sector and enterprises incorporated under public law;
in GB, a general term)

261 **Eigenkapitalausstattung** f. einer öffentlichen Unternehmung
(Mittel, die von den öffentlichen Gemeinwesen einem öffentlich-rechtlichen Unternehmen oder einer *Holding* als Kapital zur Verfügung gestellt werden)

= public dividend capital

(in GB, capital made available by the Government to state-owned public enterprises, in equity form)

262 **Eigenkapital** n.

= owner's equity; shareholders funds

263 **marktübliche Verzinsung** f. des Eigenkapitals

= market rate of return on equity

264 **Fremdkapital** n.
(Verbindlichkeiten)

= borrowings; external capital
(liabilities)

265 **Gemeinnützigkeitszwecke** mpl.
(in Deutschland:
Ein Unternehmen verfolgt gemeinnützige Zwecke, wenn seine Tätigkeit darauf gerichtet ist, die Allgemeinheit auf materiellem, geistigem oder sittlichem Gebiet selbstlos zu fördern; § 52 der Abgabeordnung; in Großbritannien gesetzlich nicht definiert.)

± charitable purposes
(in Germany:
An enterprise pursues charitable purposes if its activity is directed in a disinterested manner towards the advancement of the public interest in material, spiritual and moral matters; in GB not a term defined in law.)

265a **Steuerbegünstigung** f. für gemeinnützige Zwecke

= tax concessions for charitable purposes

266 **Abgeltung** f. **gemeinwirtschaftlicher Lasten**
(Betriebskosten, die im Rahmen der Verpflichtung zur Wahrung eines gewissen Versorgungsniveaus im öffentlichen Interesse entstehen, z.B.
– ermäßigte Fahrpreise für Schüler
– Zurverfügungstellung von unrentablem örtlichem Personenverkehr auf der Schiene)

± compensation for public service obligations
(operating costs which arise in consequence of obligations to provide a certain standard of service in the public interest e.g.
– reduced fares for school children
– provision of uneconomic local railway passenger services)

267 **Erstattungspflicht** f.

= legal duty to compensate

268 **betriebsfremde Lasten** fpl.

= externally imposed obligations

269 **direkte Förderung** f.

± direct subsidy

	(aus Haushaltsmitteln)		(from public funds)
	indirekte Förderung f.	=	**indirect subsidy**
	(durch Steuervergünstigungen)		(through tax concessions)
	öffentliche Förderung f.	=	**public subsidy**
270	**Zuschuß** m.	=	**subsidy**
	Verlustzuschuß m.	=	**deficit subsidy**
	Zuschuß m. **zur Deckung von Betriebsverlusten**	=	**subsidy to cover the losses of an enterprise**
	Zuschuß m. **zur Deckung von Sonderlasten** (Ausgleichszahlung)	=	**subsidy to meet special obligations**
	Investitionszuschuß m.	=	**investment subsidy**
	Kapitalzuschuß m.	=	**capital grant (subsidy)**
	Zuschuß m. **(Subvention** f.**) für laufende Betriebskosten**	=	**revenue grant (subsidy)**
271	**freifinanzierter Wohnungsbau** m.	±	**free-market construction of housing**
272	**öffentlich geförderter Wohnungsbau** m.	±	**housing subsidized by public funds**
273	**Kostenmiete** f.	=	**cost-rent**
	(Miete auf Kostenbasis kalkuliert, unter Berücksichtigung der Bau- und Finanzierungskosten)		(rent calculated to cover costs of financing and constructing the dwelling)
274	**Objektförderung** f.	±	**subsidy on dwelling construction**
	Subjektförderung f. (Wohngeld)	±	**housing benefit paid to an individual**
275	**Aufwendungshilfen** fpl.	±	**grant to organizations providing housing with public subsidy**
276	**finanzielle Subventionierung** f.	=	**financial support**
277	**Abgabe** f.	±	**levy**
	(umfassende Bezeichnung für Steuern, Gebühren, Beiträge)		(general expression for taxes, statutory charges and compulsory contributions)
278	**Abgabenordnung** f.	±	**fiscal law**
	(gesetzliche Rahmenregelung für Abgaben)		(legal framework for any kind of levy)
279	**Umlage** f.	±	**precept**
	(Beitrag der Verbandsmitglieder zur Deckung des Finanzbedarfs des Zweckverbands)		(contribution by member authorities to the operating costs of a joint board of similar organization)

280 **Ertrag m. der Hebesätze**
(in GB:
Ertrag aus Erhebung gemeindlicher Grundsteuer auf Grundstückswerte;
in Deutschland:
gemeindliche Zuschläge auf Gewerbesteuer)

± rate product
(in GB:
rate poundage multiplied by rateable value – in local government finance;
in Germany:
used in connection with locally determined supplements to Local Business Tax)

281 **Gebühr f.**
Benutzungsgebühr f.
(öffentlich-rechtliche Gegenleistung für die Benutzung öffentlicher Einrichtungen)

= statutory charge
± statutory charge for usage
(made under statutory authority for the use of public facilities)

282 **Tarif m.**
(privatrechtliches Entgelt für eine öffentliche Leistung, das von der vorgesetzen Behörde festgesetzt wurde)

= tariff
(payment made under private law for the use of a public service)

283 **Tarifgestaltung f.**

= tariff structure

284 **Sozialtarife mpl.**
(für bestimmte Bevölkerungsgruppen)

= concessionary tariff
(for particular groups of the population)

285 **Gebührenanstalt f.**
(Anstalt, deren Ausgaben durch Gebühren ausgeglichen werden)

± fee-charging institution
(any public institution whose expenses are met by fees and charges)

286 **Entgelt n.**
(privatrechtliche Gegenleistung für eine öffentliche Leistung)

± commercial charge
(made for the use of a public service)

287 **Beitrag m.**
Sozialversicherungsbeitrag m.
Erschließungsbeitrag m.;
Anliegerbeitrag m.
(z.B. Abwässer, Wasser, Gas)

= compulsory contribution
= social security contribution
= contribution paid for connecting a new development to public utility
(e.g. sewage, water, gas)

288 **Besteuerung f. öffentlicher Unternehmen (Betriebe)**

± taxation of public enterprises

289 **steuerliche Gewinnermittlung f.**

± determination of taxable profits by the fiscal authorities

290	Steuerbefreiung f.	=	tax exemption
291	Steuerprivileg n. öffentlicher Unternehmen	=	tax privileges of public enterprises
292	Steuerbegünstigung f. Steuerermäßigung f.	= =	tax concession tax reduction
293	Gewinnsteuern fpl.; Ertragssteuern fpl. (vermindern den ablieferungsfähigen Gewinn, insbesondere Körperschaftssteuer)	±	profits taxes (reduce net profits)
294	Körperschaftssteuer f.	±	corporation tax
295	Kostensteuern fpl. (vermindern den Gewinn)	≠	 tp.: taxes on costs (reduce gross profit)
296	steuerbegünstigter Wohnungsbau m.	±	housing construction promoted by tax concessions
297	Ertragsziele npl.	=	financial objectives
298	Geschäftsergebnis n.	=	commercial performance
299	vorgegebene Ertragsziele npl.	=	financial targets
300	≠ Üv.: (ministeriell) vorgeschriebener Mindestertrag m. (In GB wird dieser von der Regierung zur Sicherung der Effizienz öffentlicher Investitionsmittel vorgegeben. In Deutschland gibt es keinen vorgeschriebenen Mindestertrag für öffentliche Unternehmen. Wünschenswert ist generell die Sicherung der Eigenwirtschaftlichkeit.)		**required rate of return (RRR)** (In GB the required rate of return is set by the government as an efficiency measure for public investment. In Germany no required rate of return is set for public enterprises; their general aim is to break even.)
301	Verzinsung f. des Eigenkapitals, marktübliche	=	**interest payments** (nominal) **on owner's equity, at market rates**
302	interner Zins(satz) m.	=	**internal rate of return**
303	anzustrebender Betriebsertrag m.	=	**target rate of return**

304	**Diskontierungssatz** m. (Abzinsungsfaktor)	=	discount rate
305	**vorgeschriebener Diskontierungssatz** m. (Abzinsungsfaktor)	=	test discount rate
306	**diskontierter *Cash Flow*** m. (abgezinster) (abgezinster Barwert zukünftiger Erträge)	=	discounted cash flow (DCF)
307	**Nettogegenwartswert** m.; **Barwert** m. (diskontierter)	=	net present value (NPV)
308	**Kosten-Nutzen-Analyse** f.	=	cost benefit analysis
309	**Kostenwirksamkeitsanalyse** f.	=	cost effectiveness analysis
310	**Standardisierung** f. **von Zinssätzen**	=	normalization of interest rates
311	**Ausgabebeschränkungen** fpl.	=	cash limits on spending in nominal terms
	(im Sinne von Baraufwendungen in laufenden Preisen) (in Deutschland im Gegensatz zu indossierten Kreditbeschaffungspreisen; in GB für Ministerien, kommunale Behörden und öffentliche [staatliche] Unternehmen)		(as opposed to the use of resources in volume terms) (in Germany spending out of cash resources as opposed to credit-financed spending; in GB for Ministries, local authorities and public enterprises of the State)
312	**Begrenzung** f. **der Kreditaufnahme**	=	External Financing Limits (EFL)
	(ministeriell vorgeschriebene) (in GB Begrenzung der Kreditaufnahme der öffentlichen Unternehmen [diese erfolgt meist beim Finanzministerium]; in Deutschland gibt es keine formelle direkte Begrenzung der Kreditaufnahme für öffentliche Unternehmen; allenfalls bestehen indirekte Begrenzungen durch Regeln zur Einhaltung einer gewissen Proportion zwischen Eigen- und Fremdkapital.)		(in GB set by the government as a limit to borrowing by public enterprises [mostly from the Exchequer]; in Germany borrowing by public enterprises is not directly limited; there are, however, indirect limits set by regulations aiming at a certain relation of owner's equity to external capital.)

313	Kapitalrationierung f. (im Rahmen des Haushalts)	=	capital rationing
314	Prioritätsansetzung f. bei Investitionsvorhaben	=	merit order system
315	in Geldwert gemessene Leistung f.	=	Value for Money (VFM)
316	Effizienzstudien fpl.	=	efficiency studies
317	Investitionsprogramme npl. Genehmigung f. von Investitionsprogrammen	= =	investment programmes approval of ~ ~
318	Überprüfung f. von Investitionsprogrammen	=	investment review
319	Investitionsprogramme npl. Korrektur f. von Investitionsprogrammen	= =	investment programmes adjustment to ~ ~
320	Wirtschaftsplan m.	±	corporate plan
321	mehrjährige Unternehmensplanung f.	=	rolling corporate plan
322	betrieblicher Jahresplan m.	=	annual operating plan
323	Planungsspielraum m.	=	planning margin
324	Unternehmensrisiko n.	=	entrepreneurial risk
325	Finanzplanung f.	±	financial forecasting
326	Mittelverwendung f.	=	use of resources
327	Vermögensplan m.; Finanzplan m.	±	projected use of assets
328	Anschaffungskosten pl.; Herstellungskosten pl.	=	production costs
329	Löhne mpl. und Gehälter npl.	=	wages and salaries
330	soziale Abgaben fpl.	=	social security contributions
331	Erlöse mpl. und Kosten pl.	=	profit and cost account for a specific cost centre

332	Erfolgsplan m.	±	profit and loss forecast
333	Erfolgsrechnung f.	±	profit and loss account
334	Preispolitik f. für öffentliche Unternehmen (Grenzkosten; Durchschnittskosten; gespaltener Tarif; Spitzentarifierung; gibt es in Deutschland nur für Bundesbahn und Bundespost)	±	pricing policies of nationalized industries (marginal cost; average cost; multi-part tariff; peak-load tariff; exist in Germany only for the Federal Railways and the Federal Post Office)
335	Preisdämpfungsfunktion f.	±	using public enterprises to hold down prices in a particular sector of the economy
336	Ausgleichsklausel f.	±	index-linking of prices in contracts
337	Kostendeckung f.	=	recovery of costs
	Kostendeckungsprinzip n.	=	principle of recovering costs
	Kostendeckungsgrad m.	=	the extent to which costs are recovered
	Teilkostendeckung f.	=	partial recovery of costs
	Kostenechtheit f. der Preise (öffentlicher Leistungen)	=	the extent to which prices (of public services) reflect true costs
338	Poolabkommen n.	=	pooling arrangement
339	Sonderabmachungen fpl.	=	charging agreements; agreed charges
340	Durchschnittskosten pl.	=	average costs
341	Grenzkosten pl.	=	marginal costs
	langfristige Grenzkosten pl	=	long-run marginal costs
342	Zuschlag m.	=	surcharge
343	Vollkostenprinzip n.	=	full cost pricing
344	Kontrolle f.	±	control; audit
345	Vorkontrolle f.; Rechtmäßigkeitskontrolle f.; Rechtsaufsicht f.	=	control to ensure that proposals conform to regulations
346	Nachkontrolle f.	=	post-hoc audit of activity
347	begleitende Kontrolle f.	=	concurrent audit

348	parlamentarische Kontrolle f.	=	parliamentary audit
349	**Innenrevision** f.; interne Kontrolle f.; interne Revision f.; Internrevision f. (unabhängige Kontrolle innerhalb eines Unternehmens zum Zweck der Überprüfung der Buchführung, des Finanzwesens und anderer Funktionen im Dienst der Geschäftsleitung)	±	internal audit (independent financial examination within an enterprise, to check standards of financial records, performance and other tasks as directed by management)
350	**externe Kontrolle** f. (durch Wirtschaftsprüfer, Beteiligungsverwaltung und Rechnungshof)	±	external audit (carried out by firms of auditors, or by audit commissions for central and local government)
351	**Zweckmäßigkeitskontrolle** f.	±	systems audit; control to ensure that processes and measures confirm to objectives
352	**Prüfung** f.	±	audit
353	Üv.: Institut n. für öffentliches Finanz- und Rechnungswesen, staatlich registriertes (GB) (ein Institut, das Fachnormen für die Verwaltung öffentlicher Finanzen festsetzt und überwacht)	≠	**Chartered Institute of Public Finance and Accountancy (GB)** (an institute which sets and maintains standards of competence in public sector financial managements)
354	**Rechnungshof** m.	±	**National Audit Office** (formerly Exchequer and Audit Department)
355	**(Präsident** m. **des) Rechnungshof(s)** m. (in GB praktisch Synonym für ›Rechnungshof‹) (Wenn ein Minister Geld an eine öffentliche Unternehmung zahlt oder von ihr erhält, muß er die entsprechenden Ziffern dem Präsidenten des Rechnungshofs unterbreiten; dieser wird in Großbritannien nach Maßgabe des Finanz- und Revisionsgesetzes von 1866 ernannt.)	±	**Comptroller and Auditor General** (Where a Minister pays money to or receives money from a public authority, he has to lay figures before the Comptroller and Auditor General; appointed under the Exchequer and Audit Department Act 1866)

356	Prüfungsinstanz f. für die kommunale Verwaltung	±	Audit Commission for Local Government
357	**Abschlußprüfung** f. (Prüfung des Jahresabschlusses einer Aktiengesellschaft unter Einbeziehung der Buchführung und des Geschäftsberichts durch Wirtschaftsprüfungsgesellschaften; in Deutschland: bei GmbHs bei Erreichung bestimmter Werte des Stammkapitals)	=	auditing of the annual accounts (auditing of the annual accounts of a public limited company including financial records and financial performance, by commercial auditors; in Germany: only required for private companies over a certain size equity capital)
358	**Prüfungspflicht** f. (der Wirtschaftsbetriebe der öffentlichen Hand)	±	requirement to be audited (as applied to commercial enterprises run by the public sector)
359	**Pflichtprüfung** f.	±	compulsory audit
360	**Prüfungsbericht** m. (des Wirtschaftsprüfers); **Berichterstattung** f.	±	auditor's report
361	**Prüfungsvermerk** m.; **Bestätigungsvermerk** m. eingeschränkter ~ **Einzelbeanstandung** f.	= = =	auditor's certificate qualified ~ ~ qualified comment
362	**Rechnungsprüfung** f.	=	financial audit
363	**Prüfungsergebnis** n.	=	audit outcome
364	amtlich bestellter **Rechnungsprüfer** m.	=	(official) auditor
365	**Wirtschaftsprüfer** m.	±	(commercial) auditor
366	**Wirtschaftsprüfungswesen** n.	=	accountancy (as a profession or occupation)
367	**Wirtschaftsprüfungsgesellschaft** f.	=	accountancy firm
368	**Prüfungsverband** m.	±	institute of chartered accountants
369	**Rechnungsprüfungskollegium** n.	±	audit team

370	Bewertung f. Bewertungsgrundsätze mpl. Unterbewertung f. Überbewertung f.	=	valuation = ~ principles undervaluation overvaluation
371	Buchwert m.	=	book value
372	Inflationsbuchführung f. *Sandilands*-Bericht m. zur ~	= =	inflation accounting Sandilands Report on ~ ~
373	Wertberichtigungen fpl.	=	adjustments to valuations
374	Rechnungswesen n. kaufmännisches ~ öffentliches ~	= = =	accounting business ~ public sector ~
375	Buchführung f. ordnungsgemäße ~	= =	bookkeeping correct ~
376	Kameralistik f.; kameralistische Buchführung f. (s. Einleitung 1.2)	± = 	bookkeeping within the framework of State accounting conventions cameralistics (s. Introduction 1.2)
377	erweiterte kameralistische Buchführung	±	expanded State accounting (cameralistic) system
378	Betriebskameralistik f.	±	State accounting conventions (cameralistics) used in enterprises
379	gehobene kameralistische Buchführung f. (in Deutschland: für betriebsähnliche Einrichtungen der Verwaltung und Regiebetriebe; ermöglicht Bewertung des Betriebsergebnisses durch die Betriebsabrechnung, welche Abschreibungen berücksichtigt)	±	single entry State accounting (cameralistic) system with capital entries included (in Germany: a system used in quasi-commercial and trading fund activities of public administrations; it allows evaluation of trading performance by accountancy conventions which include amortization.)
380	doppelte kaufmännische Buchführung f.; (Doppik)	=	double entry bookkeeping
381	Rohertrag m. Rohaufwand m.	= =	gross revenue gross expenditure

382	betriebsbezogene Erträge mpl.	=	revenue from the primary activity of the enterprise
383	Erträge mpl. aus Beteiligungen	=	investment income
384	Erträge mpl. aus anderen Finanzanlagen	=	income from financial deposits
385	Erträge mpl. aus dem Abgang von Gegenständen des Anlagevermögens (Immobilien)	=	income from disposals of assets
386	Verluste mpl. aus dem Abgang von Gegenständen des Anlagevermögens	=	losses from disposals of assets
387	Erträge mpl. aus der Auflösung von Rückstellungen	=	income from cancellation of reserve provisions
388	Aufwendungen fpl. (für Roh-, Hilfs- und Betriebsstoffe und für bezogene Waren)	=	expenditure (on factor inputs)
389	Jahreserfolgsrechnung f.	±	financial statement for the year
390	Geschäftsjahr n.; Wirtschaftsjahr n.	=	business year; financial year
391	Wirtschaftsperiode f.	=	business horizon
392	Jahresabschluß m. Feststellung f. des Jahresabschlusses (durch den Verwaltungsrat/Aufsichtsrat; bei Eigenbetrieben auch durch den Gemeinderat)	± =	annual accounts approval of the annual accounts (by the Executive Board/Supervisory Board)
393	Jahresbericht m.; Geschäftsbericht m.	=	Annual Report
394	Vorlage f. des Jahresberichts und Rechnungslegung	=	presentation of annual report and accounts
395	Jahresbilanz f.	±	annual balance sheet
396	Handelsbilanz f. (maßgebend für Steuerbilanz)	=	balance sheet (trading)

397	Steuerbilanz f.	=	balance sheet drawn up for taxation purposes
398	Zwischenabschluß m. (während des Geschäftsjahres)	=	interim accounts
399	Betriebsergebnis n.	=	trading result
400	Feststellung f. des Betriebsergebnisses	±	taking note of trading results (procedure at Annual General Meeting of German companies)
401	Betriebsabrechnung f.	=	summary of operating accounts
402	Investitionsrechnung f.	±	capital account
403	Erträge mpl. und Aufwendungen fpl.	=	profit and cost account
404	Kostenrechnung f.	=	cost accounting
405	Einnahmen fpl. und Ausgaben fpl.	=	income and expenditure
406	Umsatz m.	=	turnover; sales
407	Umsatzerlöse mpl.	=	turnover; sales receipts
408	Fehlbetrag m.; Defizit n.	=	deficit; shortfall
409	Bilanz f. (Aktivseite – Vermögenswerte Passivseite – Verbindlichkeiten, einschließlich Eigenkapital)	=	balance sheet (assets liabilities, including owner's equity)
410	Bilanzgewinn m. Jahresgewinn m.	= =	accounting profit; annual profit
411	Bilanzstichtag m.	=	date on which balance is struck
412	Jahresfehlbetrag m. Bilanzverlust m. Jahresverlust m.	= = =	annual deficit accounting deficit annual deficit; annual loss (deficit)
413	Ausgleich m. des Jahresverlusts (z.B. eines Eigenbetriebs) durch die Gemeinde	=	making up the deficit of a municipal enterprise

414	Vortragen n. des Jahresverlusts auf neue Rechnung	=	carrying forward a deficit
415	Überschuß m.	=	surplus
416	Jahresüberschuß m.	=	annual surplus
417	Gewinn m. ~ erzielen	= =	profit to make a ~
418	Gewinn- und Verlustrechnung f.	=	profit and loss accounting
419	Gewinn-/Verlustvortrag m. aus dem Vorjahr	=	profit/loss carried forward from the previous year
420	Vortragen n. des Jahresgewinns auf neue Rechnung	=	carrying forward a profit
421	Scheingewinn m. (z.B. aufgrund von unzureichenden Abschreibungen)	=	apparent profit (e.g. because of insufficient provision for depreciation)
422	Gewinnablieferung f.	=	transfer of profits; ~ ~ surplus
423	ablieferungsfähiger Gewinn m.	=	transferable profits; ~ surplus
424	Rücklage f. Rücklagekapital n. eine Rücklage bilden eine Rücklage auflösen einer Rücklage Mittel entnehmen Rücklageentnahme f. stille Reserven fpl. Einstellung f. aus dem Jahresüberschuß in offene Rücklagen	= = = = = = = =	capital reserve reserve fund to build up a reserve to release a reserve; to wind up a reserve fund to draw from reserves withdrawal from reserves undeclared reserves transferring trading surplus to reserves
425	Rückstellung f.	±	reserve provision
426	offene Rücklagen fpl. freie Rücklagen fpl. gesetzliche Rücklagen fpl.	= = =	declared reserves free and untrammeled reserves statutorily required reserves; legally required reserves
427	Aufwendungen fpl. für Altersversorgung und Unterstützung	=	provision for pensions and social support payments

428 **Pensionsrückstellungen** fpl. = **provision for pension payments**

429 ≠ **redundancy fund reserve**
Üv.: Rückstellung f. für Abfindungen für Betriebszugehörigkeit
(für die gesetzlich vorgeschriebene Entschädigung von Arbeitnehmern bei Beendigung des Arbeitsverhältnisses) (provision for statutory redundancy payments)

430 **Rechnungsabgrenzungsposten** mpl. = **deferred liabilities**
(item applicable to a future accounting period)

431 **Aufwendungen** fpl. **aus Verlustübernahme** = **meeting the cost of acquired liabilities**

432 **Sonderrechnung** f. = **separate accounts**
(eines aus der öffentlichen Verwaltung ausgegliederten Betriebs) (of an enterprise which has been separated from local authority administration)

433 **Nettoetatisierung** f. = **budgeting on a net basis**
(Eigenbetriebe und bestimmte Regiebetriebe erscheinen im Haushaltsplan der Gebietskörperschaft lediglich mit dem Zuschuß der Gebietskörperschaft oder mit der Ablieferung an die Gebietskörperschaft. Zuschuß bzw. Ablieferung können in verschiedenen Formen geleistet werden.) (Municipal enterprises and certain trading fund activities may appear in local authority accounts only in terms of the surplus being transferred to the authority or the net subsidy required.)

434 **Ausgliederung** f. = **separation**

435 **rechnungsmäßige Ausgliederung** f. **des Eigenbetriebs aus der Kommunalverwaltung** = **separation for accounting purposes of a municipal enterprise from local authority administration**

436 **ausgegliederte Verwaltung** f. = **autonomous management**

437 **Vergabewesen** n.; **Beschaffungswesen** n. = **procurement system**

438 **Politik** f. **des öffentlichen Auftragswesens (Vergabewesens)** = **public purchasing policy; public procurement**

439 **Vergabe** f. = **placing; letting out**

	∼ von öffentlichen Aufträgen	=	∼ of public contracts
	∼ von öffentlichen Bauleistungen	=	∼ of public construction work
	∼ von Lieferungen	=	∼ of supply contracts
440	Vergabeart f.	=	contracts procedure
441	Verdingungsordnung f. für Leistungen, ausgenommen Bauleistungen (VOL)	±	standard terms and conditions for the supply of goods and services to public bodies
442	Verdingungsordnung f. für Bauleistungen (VOB)	±	standard building contracts in the public sector
443	öffentliche Ausschreibung f.	=	public invitation to tender
444	eingeschränkte Ausschreibung f.	=	restricted invitation to tender
	eingeschränkte Ausschreibung f. mit öffentlichem Teilnahmewettbewerb	=	restricted invitation to tender with public competition from an approved list
445	freihändige Vergabe f.	=	award of contract by private agreement

6.4 Energiewirtschaft
(in Deutschland ohne Kohle)

Energy Industries
(in GB Coal, Gas, Electricity, Nuclear Power, Hydroelectric Power)

446	Primärenergie f.	=	primary energy
	Sekundärenergie f.	=	secondary energy
447	Primärenergieversorgung f.	=	primary fuel industries
	Sekundärenergieversorgung f.	=	secondary fuel industries
448	Energiepolitik f. (für Brennstoffe)	=	fuel policy
449	Energiewirtschaft f. (in Großbritannien: enthält im weitesten Sinne auch den Kohlebergbau und Erdölproduktion)	=	the energy industries (in Great Britain: in its broadest sense, includes coal mining and oil production)
450	Energieverbund m.	=	integration of energy systems
451	Energieeinsparung f.	=	energy conservation

452	Energieversorgungsunternehmen n. (EVU) (produziert und/oder verteilt Elektrizität, Gas, Fernwärme)	=	energy supply undertaking (produces and/or distributes electricity, gas, district heating)
453	Energieverteilungsnetz n.	=	energy distribution network
454	Kraft-Wärmekopplung f. (Kopplung der Produktion von Strom und Wärme)	=	combined heat and power (CHP)
455	Fernwärme f.; Fernheizung f.	=	district heating
456	Demarkationsvertrag m. (dient der gegenseitigen Abgrenzung der Versorgungsgebiete von EVU)	=	demarcation agreement (defines boundaries of supply areas for energy undertakings)
457	zentrale Stromerzeugungsanstalt f. (öffentliches Stromerzeugungsmonopol in England und Wales)	=	Central Electricity Generating Board (CEGB) (public generating monopoly for England and Wales)
458	Verband m. Deutscher Elektrizitätswerke (VDEW) (in GB: gesetzliche Dachorganisation zur Überwachung der Stromverteilungsanstalten; in Deutschland: freier Verband)	±	Electricity Council (in GB, an official body which oversees the electricity industry; in Germany, voluntary association of electricity utilities)
459	regionale Stromverteilungsanstalten fpl.	=	area boards for electricity distribution
460	Stromversorgungsnetz n. für das gesamte Staatsgebiet	=	national grid
461	Kraftwerk n. Speicherkraftwerk n. Wasserkraftwerk n. Wärmekraftwerk n. Kernkraftwerk n.	= = = = =	power station pumped storage ~ ~ hydroelectric ~ ~ thermal ~ ~ nuclear ~ ~ LWR – Light Water Reactor AGR – Advanced Gascooled Reactor PWR – Pressurized Water Reactor SGHWR – Steam Generating Heavy Water Reactor

462	Gezeitenenergie f.	=	tidal energy
463	Gezeitenstauwerk n.	=	estuarial barrage
464	Verstromung f. (von Kohle in Elektrizität)	=	conversion to electricity (e.g. of coal)
465	Hochspannungsleitung f. Niederspannungsleitung f.	= =	high tension electricity supply cable low tension electricity supply cable
466	Grundlast f. Spitzenlast f.	= =	base load peak load
467	Spitzenzeiten fpl.	=	peak periods
468	Auslastungsfaktor m.	=	load factor
469	Spitzenlastdauerkurve f.	=	load duration curve
470	Kapazitätsauslastung f. der Anlagen	=	plant loading
471	Abschaltung f. von Abnehmern wegen Netzüberlastung	=	load-shedding
472	gleichzeitige Spitzenbelastung f. (des Elektrizitätsnetzes)	=	simultaneous maximum demand (on the electricity supply grid)
473	Haushaltstarif m. Gewerbetarif m. Sondertarif m.	= = =	domestic tariff industrial tariff negotiated tariff
474	Abnehmer m. Tarifabnehmer m. Sonderabnehmer m.	= = =	consumer ∼ on standard tariff ∼ by negotiated price
475	gespaltener Tarif m. (Kostenträgerrechnung: Tarifkunden Sonderabnehmer Sondervertragskunden)	= = = =	multi-part tariff (based on calculation of costs related to user categories: tariff customers special users special contract customers)
476	Pauschaltarif m. für Stromabgabe an Elektrizitätsversorgungsunternehmen (für die Verteilung des Stroms)	=	bulk supply tariff

477	unterbrechbare Belieferungsverträge mpl. (bei Gas für industrielle Zwecke)	=	interruptible supplies contracts (in industrial gas supply)
478	flüssiges Erdgas n.	=	liquid natural gas (LNG)
479	Anlandungspreis m. für Nordsee-Erdgas	=	beachhead price of gas
480	Erdgas-/Rohöl-Preis m. ab Bohrloch (Förderungsort)	=	well-head price of gas/oil
481	Zechenstillegung f. von unwirtschaftlichen Betrieben	=	pit closures; elimination of uneconomic mining capacity
482	Kohlepfennig m. (in Deutschland: wird vom Verbraucher mit dem Strompreis gezahlt und zur Finanzierung der Förderung des Einsatzes von Steinkohle in Kraftwerken eingesetzt)	≠	tp.: coal *Pfennig* (in Germany: impost on electricity users to finance state subsidies on the use of coal in power stations)
483	Inspektion f. (für z.B. nukleare Einrichtungen)	±	H.M. Inspectorates (e.g. Nuclear Installations Inspectorate)
484	Verglasung f. von Atommüll	=	vitrification of nuclear waste

6.5 Sonstige Versorgungswirtschaft
Wasserversorgung
Abwasserentsorgung
Post
Fernmeldewesen

Supply of other Essential Services
Water Supply
Sewage Disposal
Postal Services
Telecommunications

485	Wasserversorgungs- und Abwasseranstalten fpl. (in Deutschland oft regionale Zweckverbände; in GB auch zuständig für Kanalisationsanlagen für Abwässer)	±	Regional Water Authorities (in Germany often also regional bodies; in GB responsible for water supply, drainage and sewage disposal)

486	Wasserverbund m.	=	integrated water supply system
487	Entsorgung f.	±	sewage and refuse disposal services
	Abfallbeseitigung f.; Müllabfuhr f.	=	solid wastes disposal
	Müllverbrennung f.	=	incineration of solid waste
	Müllverbrennungsanlage f.	=	solid waste incinerator
	Straßenreinigung f.	=	street cleansing
	Entwässerung f.	=	sewage disposal
	Abwasserbeseitigung f.	=	waste water disposal
	Klärwerk n.; Kläranlage f.	=	sewage works
	Kernenergieentsorgung f.	=	radioactive waste disposal
488	Anschlußzwang m.	=	compulsory connection
	Benutzungszwang m.	=	~ usage

(Gemeinden können aus Gründen des öffentlichen Wohles durch Satzung den Anschluß der in der Gemeinde gelegenen Grundstücke an die gemeindliche Wasserleitung, Kanalisation, Müllabfuhr, Straßenreinigung etc. vorschreiben [Anschlußzwang]. Sie können weiter die Benutzung dieser und weiterer Einrichtungen, z.B. des Schlachthofs, zur Pflicht machen [Benutzungszwang].)

(Local authorities may, in the public interest, require through bye-law that developments on land in their area be connected to water supply and sewerage and that provision is made for refuse disposal and street cleansing [compulsory connection]. They can also make the use of these facilities, and of others [e.g. municipal abattoir], compulsory [compulsory usage].)

489 ≠
Üv.: Amt n. für Telekommunikation (OFTEL)
(in Großbritannien 1984 geschaffen zur Regulierung des Telekommunikationssektors nach Privatisierung von *British Telecom*)

Office of Telecommunications (OFTEL)

(a body established in 1984 to regulate the telecommunications sector after the privatization of British Telecom)

489a ≠
Üv.: Amt n. für Gasversorgung *(OFGAS)*
(Amt zur Regelung der Gasversorgung nach der Privatisierung der *British Gas Corporation* 1986)

OFGAS

(a body established in 1986 to regulate the gas supply industry after the privatization of the British Gas Corporation [British Gas PLC])

6.6 Verkehrswirtschaft
    Schienenverkehr
    Straßenverkehr
    Hafenwirtschaft
    Wasserstraßen

Transport Industries
Rail
Air
Road
Ports
Waterways

490	Verkehrswirtschaft f. Versorgungswirtschaft f.	=	transport sector public utilities
491	öffentlicher Verkehr m. (im Gegensatz zu Werkverkehr)	=	public transport (as opposed to personal transport or transport on own account)
492	Verkehrsunternehmen npl.; Verkehrsbetriebe mpl.	=	transport undertakings
493	Verkehrsunternehmen npl. (im Eigentum) der öffentlichen Hand	=	public transport undertakings (publicly owned)
494	öffentlicher Personalverkehr m.	=	local public passenger transport
495	Personenbeförderungsfall m.	=	passenger journey
496	Personenverkehrsbehörde f.	=	passenger transport authority (PTA)
497	Personenverkehrsbetriebe m. in Großstädten	=	passenger transport executive (PTE)
498	Individualverkehr m. (z.B. Pkw)	=	individual traffic (e.g. by car)
499	Beförderungspflicht f.	=	common carrier obligation
500	Erstattung f. (Zuschüsse mpl.) für nichtkostendeckende Personenverkehrslinien	=	grants for unremunerative passenger services (Section 29 Transport Act 1968)
501	Verkehrsverbund m.	=	integrated transport system
502	Verkehrstarife mpl. Einheitstarif m. (unabhängig von der Entfernung) Leistungstarif m. Zonentarif m.	=	transport tariffs standard fare; ~ price (irrespective of distance) level of performance tariff zoned tariff

	Teilstreckentarif m.	=	staged tariff
	Kilometertarif m.	=	tariff per kilometre
	Ermäßigungstarif m.	=	concessionary tariff
	Verbundtarif m.	=	integrated fare structure

| 503 | Fernverkehr m. | = | long-distance traffic |
| | Nahverkehr m. | = | local traffic |

504	Nutzwagenkilometer m.	=	vehicle kilometres
	Sitzkilometer m.	=	seat kilometres
	Personenkilometer m.	=	passenger kilometres

505 Sitzkapazitätenauslastung f. = seating load factor

506 ≠ Traffic Commissioners
Üv.: (in GB) Fachaufsichtsbehörde f.
(für gewerblichen Straßenverkehr (in GB supervise and licence commer-
[Autobusse und Lkws]) cial road haulage and public road
transport)

507 ≠ Traffic Areas
Üv.: Bezirke mpl. der Fachauf- (in GB areas for which the Traffic
sichtsbehörden für gewerblichen Commissioners are responsible)
Straßenverkehr (in GB)

508 Flugsicherungsanstalt f. ± Air Traffic Control Service

509 Wegekostenrechnung f. = transport cost calculation

510 Wegekosten pl. = track costs

511 Verkehrswegeerhaltung f. = track maintenance

6.7 Verarbeitende Industrien als öffentliche Unternehmen

Manufacturing Industries Owned As Public Enterprises

512 ≠
Üv.: Königliche Waffenfabrik f. Royal Ordnance Factories
(in GB) (in GB)

513 Absatzgesellschaften fpl., = Agricultural Marketing Boards
landwirtschaftliche (e.g. milk, wool) in GB
(in GB; genossenschaftsähnliche)

6.8 Kommunale Unternehmen — Municipal Enterprises

514 **kommunale Wirtschaft** f.
(wirtschaftliche Betätigung der Gemeinde)

= **municipal enterprise**
(economic activities of a local authority)

515 **kommunaler Betrieb** m.

= **municipal undertaking**

516 **Gemeinderat** m.

= **municipal council**

517 **Kommunalaufsicht** f.
(in der Bundesrepublik: Aufgabe der Länder;
in GB: Zuständigkeit des Umweltministeriums, des Amtes für *Wales* und des Amtes für Schottland)

= **supervision of local authority affairs**
(in Germany: a *Land* Government function;
in GB: Department of Environment, Welsh Office, Scottish Office)

518 **Haushaltssatzung** f.

= **budget regulations**

519 **Gemeindehaushalt** m.
(in Deutschland:
bestehend aus dem Verwaltungshaushalt [laufende Einnahmen und Ausgaben] und dem Vermögenshaushalt [vermögenswirksame Einnahmen und Ausgaben, insbesondere für Investitionen und die Aufnahme und Tilgung von Krediten];
in Großbritannien:
Der Gemeindehaushalt weist aus laufende Einnahmen und Ausgaben [die zu etwa 50% aus Finanzanweisungen des Staates bestehen] und vermögenswirksame Aufwendungen [die aus Anleihen und Veräußerungen gedeckt werden].
Die formellen Regeln für den Gemeindehaushalt und das kommunale Rechnungswesen werden in der Haushaltssatzung vom Staat festgelegt.)

= **local authority budget**
(in Germany:
consists of an administrative budget [revenue receipts and expenditure] and a capital budget [capital receipts and expenditure, especially for investment items and the floating and servicing of loans];

in Great Britain:
A local authority budget consists of income and expenditure on revenue account [financed approximately 50% from government grants] and of expenditure on capital account [financed by borrowing but also by capital receipts].
The general form of local authority budgets and accounts are specified by government regulations.)

520 **Querverbund** m.
(von kommunalen Unternehmen)
(in Deutschland:
Zusammenfassung verschiedener kommunaler Unternehmen, z.B.

± **revenue pooling**
(in municipal undertakings)
(in Germany:
pooling of revenue from different local authority utility and transport

von Versorgungsbetrieben oder von Versorgungsbetrieben mit Verkehrsbetrieben, wobei die Überschüsse des einen Betriebs zum Ausgleich des Defizits eines anderen Betriebs dienen;
in Großbritannien:
im allgemeinen nicht zugelassen; seit dem *Transport Act* von 1985 müssen kommunale Busunternehmen als Aktiengesellschaften errichtet werden.)

undertakings so that surpluses from one undertaking can balance deficits in another;

Revenue pooling is not generally permitted in Britain. Under the Transport Act 1985, municipal bus undertakings will have to be set up as limited companies.)

521 **Stadtwerke** fpl.
(in Deutschland:
Zusammenfassung kommunaler Verkehrs- und Versorgungsleistungen in einem Unternehmen;
in Großbritannien:
in den größeren Städten Ämter für technische Dienste)

± **municipal undertaking**
(in Germany:
grouping of local authority transport and utility provisions in a single undertaking;
in Great Britain:
Departments of Technical Services in the larger cities are the nearest equivalent)

522 **Eigenbetrieb** m.
(in Deutschland:
verselbständigter Regiebetrieb, nichtrechtsfähiges wirtschaftliches Unternehmen vor allem der Gemeinden; erscheint im Haushalt des Trägers nur netto, d.h. mit der Zuführung oder Ablieferung, z.B. Verkehrs- oder Versorgungsunternehmen)

± **autonomous (local) undertaking**
(in Germany:
operationally autonomous trading fund activity devoid of legal personality, most commonly found among local authorities; only its net financial results appear in the budget of its owning body, i.e. surplus or deficit e.g. of public transport undertaking.)

523 **Eigenbetriebsgesetz** n.;
Eigenbetriebsverordnung f.
(in Deutschland:
letztere ersetzt durch die Eigenbetriebsgesetze der Länder;

in Großbritannien:
Ähnliche Aktivitäten werden auf verschiedenen Rechtswegen kontrolliert.)

± **bye-laws; regulations governing the affairs of local undertakings**
(in Germany:
bye-laws relating to autonomous local enterprises [now replaced by *Land* legislation];
in Great Britain:
Similar activities are regulated through a variety of legislative means.)

524 **Träger** m.;
Trägerverband m.

= **owner;
owners**

115

	(Zweckverband; Konsortium)		(joint board of local authorities; consortium)
			consortium = non-legal term in GB
	(s. Nr. 112, 146)		(s. Nos. 112, 146)
525	Üv.: kommunale Kreditagenturen fpl.	≠	local enterprise boards
	(Investitionskreditfonds einiger kommunaler Behörden in Großbritannien aus kommunalen Abgaben oder Pensionsfonds finanziert, zur Kreditgewährung oder Beteiligung an privaten gewerblichen Unternehmen in deren Einzugsgebiet)		(investment agencies established by some local authorities in Great Britain, with capital from the rates or from local government pension funds, to make loans or equity payments to private-sector industrial enterprises in their locality)
526	städtischer Wohnungsbesitz m.	=	municipal housing stock
527	städtische Wohnungsbaugesellschaft f.	±	municipal housing undertakings
	(in Deutschland: meist Kapitalgesellschaften; in Großbritannien: Teil der Kommunalverwaltung)		(in Germany: normally established as companies; in Great Britain: form part of local authority administration)
528	gemeinnütziges Wohnungsunternehmen n.	±	public housing undertakings
	(umfaßt in Großbritannien städtische Wohnungsabteilungen, eingetragene Wohnungsvereine und Körperschaften für neue Siedlungen)		(In Great Britain the term encompasses municipal housing departments, registered housing associations and new town corporations.)
529	Wohnungswirtschaft f.	=	housing
	gemeinnützige ~	=	public sector ~
530	Planung f. (ohne Zusatz meist physische); Bauleitplanung f.	=	planning
531	Abnahme f. (von Bauleistungen oder Lieferungen)	±	certification (of completion of work)
532	direkte Arbeitsgruppenorganisation f.	±	direct labour organization (DLO)
	(s. Nr. 118a; in GB praktisch Regiebetrieb;		(s. No. 118a; municipal work force primarily to re-

kommunaler Arbeitsbetrieb vorwiegend für Reparationen, hat manchmal den Charakter einer Bau- oder Konstruktionsfirma. Neuregelungen seit 1980 haben diese Institution mehr betriebswirtschaftlich-wettbewerbsmäßig ausgerichtet.)

pair council property but, in some cases, taking on the characteristics of a construction or civil engineering enterprise.
Regulations under the Local Government, Planning and Land Act 1980 have placed DLO arrangements on a more commercial and competitive basis.)

533 **Betriebsführungsvertrag** m.

(z.B. Müllabfuhr, Kinderheime)

± **private sector provision of local authority services under contract**
(e.g. refuse collection, children's homes)

534 **Bezugsvertrag** m.
(mit einem fremden Versorgungsunternehmen zur Belieferung des gemeindlichen Versorgungsbetriebs, der weiterverteilt)

= **delivery contract**
(when a local authority undertaking accepts bulk supplies for local distribution)

6.9 Arbeitsrecht und Personalpolitik

Labour Law And Manpower Issues

535 **Arbeitgeber-Arbeitnehmer-Verhältnis** npl.
(Beziehungen zwischen Arbeitgebern und Gewerkschaften bzw. Sozialpartnern)

= **industrial relations**
(relationships between employers and trade unions or other negotiating bodies)

536 **Tarifvertrag** m.

(in Deutschland:
schriftlicher Vertrag zwischen einem Arbeitgeber oder Arbeitgeberverband und einer oder mehreren Gewerkschaften zur Regelung von arbeitsrechtlichen Rechten und Pflichten der Tarifvertragsparteien und zur Festsetzung von Rechtsnormen über Inhalt, Abschluß und Beendigung von Arbeitsverhältnissen sowie über betriebliche Fragen; in Großbritannien ist der gesetzliche Rahmen von Tarifverträgen weniger klar umrissen. Im allge-

± **wages and conditions agreement; collective agreement**
(in Germany:
written agreement between an employer or employers association and one or more trade unions which determines the rights and duties under labour law of the parties to the agreement and which fixes the legal framework for the content and termination of conditions of service and for other internal matters;

in Great Britain the legal framework for **collective** agreements on wages and conditions is less clearly expressed.

meinen werden die meisten britischen Arbeiter von den Gerichten angehalten, ihre eigenen Arbeitsverträge abzuschließen.)

In general, most British workers are held by the Courts to have **individual** contracts of employment.)

537 **Betriebsvereinbarung** f.;
im öffentlichen Dienst:
Dienstvereinbarung f.

(Vertrag, der schriftlich für einen Betrieb zwischen Arbeitgeber und Betriebsrat für Arbeitsverhältnisse sowie über betriebliche Fragen geschlossen wird)

± **agreement at the level of the enterprise**

(written agreement between the management of an enterprise and the works council which fixes the framework for conditions of service and other internal matters)

538 **Arbeitsdirektor** m.

(in Deutschland:
in Unternehmen mit Mitbestimmung; der Arbeitsdirektor wird von der Belegschaft gewählt und ist als Vorstandsmitglied zuständig für Personal- und Sozialfragen.)

≠
tp.: Director of Personnel
(in enterprises which have co-determination; the Director of Personnel is an employee-nominated member of the management team responsible for personnel and social questions.)

539 **Einstellung** f. **von Personal**
Entlassung f. **von Personal**
Arbeitsverhältnisse npl.
Arbeitsvertrag m.
Gewinnbeteiligung f.
Deputat n.
(Naturallohn, Teil des Arbeitslohns)
übertarifliche Leistung f.
außertarifliche Leistung f.
betriebliche Sonderleistung f.
insb. für leitende Angestellte

= **recruitment of personnel**
= **dismissal of personnel**
= **conditions of service**
= **contract of employment**
= **profit-sharing**
= **wages in kind**

= **payments "above the going rate"**
= **enhanced conditions of service**
= **enhanced "fringe benefit"**

540 **Beteiligung** f. **der Belegschaft**

= **participation of the work force**

541 **Mitbestimmung** f.
betriebliche ~

(durch den Betriebsrat)

≠
tp.: co-determination;
~ ~ at the level of the firm
(through the works council)

542 **Mitbestimmung** f. **im Unternehmen**
(in Deutschland:
Die Arbeitnehmer von Aktiengesellschaften und GmbHs mit mehr

≠
tp.: co-determination in enterprises
(in Germany:
In public limited companies, and in private companies with more than 500

als 500 Arbeitnehmern sind zu einem Drittel an den Sitzen des Aufsichtsrates beteiligt.
Das Mitbestimmungsgesetz von 1976 sieht für Gesellschaften mit i.d.R. mehr als 2000 Beschäftigten im Grundsatz die paritätische Mitbestimmung vor. Der Aufsichtsrat wird gleichmäßig durch Vertreter der Anteilseigner und der Arbeitnehmer beschickt.
Eine ähnliche Regelung gilt seit 1951 für den Bergbau und die Eisen und Stahl erzeugende Industrie [sogenannte Montan-Mitbestimmung].)

employees, the work force is entitled to one-third of the seats on the Supervisory Board.
The Co-determination Act of 1976 envisages parity of representation in all companies with more than 2000 employees, that is, the Supervisory Board would contain equal numbers representing the owners and the employees.

Similar arrangements have existed since 1951 for the coal-mining and iron and steel industries [so-called '*Montan-Mitbestimmung*'].)

543 **paritätische Mitbestimmung** f.

≠
tp.: equal co-determination

544 **überbetriebliche Mitbestimmung** f.

(von den deutschen Gewerkschaften angestrebte Beteiligung von Arbeitnehmervertretern an den Selbstverwaltungsorganen der Wirtschaft z.B. Industrie- und Handelskammern, Handwerkskammern;
als überbetriebliche Mitbestimmung kann auch die Besetzung von Aufsichtsratsposten mit Vertretern der Gewerkschaften angesehen werden.)

≠
tp.: co-determination above the level of the firm
(A situation being sought by Trade Unions in which employee representatives would be involved in the decision-making of economic umbrella bodies, e.g. chambers of commerce and industry;

co-determination above the level of the firm can also be interpreted as the nomination of trade union representatives to seats on Supervisory Boards.)

545 **Mitbestimmungsrecht** n.

(des Betriebsrats in sozialen Angelegenheiten z.B. Betriebsordnung, Arbeitszeit, Urlaubsplan)

≠
tp.: right of co-determination
(of the works council, in social matters, e.g. conditions of service, working hours, holidays)

546 **Mitwirkungsrecht** n.

(Informations- und Beratungsrecht des Betriebsrats)

≠
tp.: right of participation of the works council
(right to obtain information and give advice)

547	**Feststellung** f. **des Wirtschaftsplans** (durch den Verwaltungsrat/Werksausschuß)	=	approval of the corporate plan (by the Executive Board/Works Council)
548	**Betriebsversammlung** f.; **Personalversammlung** f.	≠	tp.: general meeting of employees
549	**Betriebsrat** m. (besteht aus gewählten Vertretern der Arbeitnehmer eines Betriebs zur Wahrnehmung ihrer Interessen gegenüber dem Arbeitgeber in betrieblichen, insbesondere sozialen, personellen und wirtschaftlichen Angelegenheiten [s. betriebliche Mitbestimmung]; geregelt im Betriebsverfassungsgesetz)	≠	tp.: works council (consists of elected representatives of the work force in an enterprise, whose function is to secure the interests of the work force within the enterprise, particularly in respect of management, personnel and social questions. The *Betriebsverfassungsgesetz* is the operating legislation.)
550	**Personalrat** m.; **Personalvertretung** f. (hat für den Bereich des öffentlichen Dienstes und der öffentlichen Betriebe, Körperschaften und Anstalten eine ähnliche Funktion wie der Betriebsrat im Bereich der Privatwirtschaft)	≠	tp.: staff council; staff association (has a similar function to the works council, in public administration and public enterprises)
551	**Beteiligungsrechte** npl. **des Betriebsrats** (in Form der Mitbestimmung und der Mitwirkung)	≠	tp.: the right of the works council to be involved (in terms of participation and co-determination)
552	**betriebliche Altersversorgung** f.	±	company pension scheme
553	**Abfindung** f. **bei Personalabbau**	=	redundancy payments
554	**Stellenübersicht** f.	±	manpower forecast
555	**Einigungsstelle** f. (wird bei Streitigkeiten zwischen Arbeitgeber und Betriebsrat gebildet)	±	arbitration commission (formed as needed to resolve conflicts between an employer and the works council)
556	**Schlichtung** f.	±	mediation
557	**Schiedsgerichtsbarkeit** f.	=	arbitration

Alphabetischer Index

(Die Ziffern hinter den Stichwörtern bezeichnen die Nummern der Wortstellen im Wortgut.)

Abfallbeseitigung **487**
Abfindung bei Personalabbau **553**
Abgabe(n) **277**, 278
Abgaben, soziale **330**
Abgabenordnung **278**
Abgeltung gemeinwirtschaftlicher Lasten **266**
Abgrenzung **259**
Abnahme (von Bauleistungen oder Lieferungen) **531**
Abnehmer **474**
Absatzgesellschaften, landwirtschaftliche **513**
Abschaltung von Abnehmern wegen Netzüberlastung **471**
Abschlußprüfung **357**
Abschlußzwang **47**
Abschreibung **243**, 379
~ auf Anschaffungskosten **243**
~ auf Wiederbeschaffungskosten **243**
~, außerplanmäßige **243**
~, nutzungsbedingte **243**
~, planmäßige **243**
~, steuerliche **243**
~, technische **243**
~, verbrauchsbedingte **243**
~, wirtschaftlich bedingte **243**
Abschreibungsfonds **246**
Abschreibungsmethoden **244**
Abwässer **287**
Abwasserbeseitigung **487**
Abzinsungsfaktor **304**, 305

Ad-hoc-Ausschuß **144**
AG 91, **95**, 186
Aktiengesellschaft 89, **95**, 132, 135, 136
Aktionäre **136**
Allgemeinheit, die ~ selbstlos fördern 265
Alternativen, verpaßte 177, 178
Altersversorgung, betriebliche **552**
Ämter für technische Dienste 521
Amt für Gasversorgung 489a
~ für Telekommunikation 489
Angehöriger des öffentlichen Dienstes 119
Angestellter, leitender **131**
Anlageänderung **232**
Anlagegüter 248
Anlagennachweis **232**
Anlagevermögen **232**
Anlandungspreis für Nordsee-Erdgas 479
Anliegerbeitrag **287**
Annahme der Rechtsform einer GmbH 68
Annuität **251**
Anschaffungskosten **328**
Anschaffungswertprinzip **242**
Anschluß- und Versorgungspflicht **47**
Anschlußzwang **488**
Anstalt, bundesunmittelbare **77**
~ (des öffentlichen Rechts) **74**, 79, 285
~, landesunmittelbare **76**

~, nichtwirtschaftliche 83
~, öffentliche **74**
Arbeitgeber 536, 537
~ – Arbeitnehmer-Verhältnisse **535**
Arbeitgeberverband 536
Arbeitnehmervertreter im Werksausschuß **142**
Arbeitsbetrieb, kommunaler **532**
Arbeitsdirektor **538**
Arbeitsgruppe im Finanzministerium zur Kontrolle öffentlicher Unternehmen 152
Arbeitsgruppenorganisation, direkte **532**
Arbeitsverhältnisse 536, 537, **539**
Arbeitsvertrag **539**
Arbeitsverträge 536
Aufgaben, öffentliche 153
Aufsicht 133
Aufsichtsbehörde **149**
Aufsichtsorgan 143
Aufsichtsrat 132, 134, **135**, 139, 392, 542
Aufsichtsrechte der Aufsichtsbehörde **149**
Auftragnehmer **61**
Aufwand 203
Aufwendungen aus Verlustübernahme **431**
~ für Altersversorgung und Unterstützung **427**
~ (für Roh-, Hilfs- und Betriebsstoffe für bezogene Waren) **388**
~, vermögenswirksame **519**

121

Aufwendungshilfen 275
Ausgabenbeschränkungen 311
Ausgaben-Planung, öffentliche 153
Ausgleich des Jahresverlusts durch die Gemeinde 413
Ausgleichsklausel 336
Ausgleichszahlung 270
Ausgliederung 434
~ des Eigenbetriebs aus der Kommunalverwaltung, rechnungsmäßige 435
Auslastungsfaktor 468
Ausschreibung, eingeschränkte 444
~, öffentliche 443
~ mit öffentlichem Teilnahmewettbewerb, eingeschränkte 444
Ausschuß 144
~ für Nationalisierung, vorbereitender 184
Außenfinanzierung 225

Bank und Handelsgesellschaft 170
Baraufwendungen in laufenden Preisen 311
Barwert, (diskontierter) 307
~ zukünftiger Erträge, abgezinster 306
Bau- oder Konstruktionsfirma 532
Bauabteilung einer Territorialverwaltung 118a
Bauleitplanung 530
Bausparkasse, öffentlich-rechtliche 209
BBC 168
Beamte und Militärpersonal 172
Beamter 171
~ einer Behörde, leitender 173

Beanstandung 149
Beanstandungsrecht 149
Beförderungspflicht 499
Befugnisse der vollziehenden Gewalt, gerichtliche 72a
Begrenzung der Kreditaufnahme 312
Beherrschung, wirtschaftliche 13
Behörde, 114, **147**
~, vorgesetzte **148**
Behörden, kommunale 311, 525
Behördenleiter **173**
Beitrag 279, **287**
Beiträge 277
Belastungen 203
Belieferungsverträge, unterbrechbare **477**
Benutzung öffentlicher Einrichtungen 281
Benutzungsgebühr **281**
Benutzungszwang **488**
Berichterstattung 360
Beschaffungswesen **437**
Beschlußorgan der Gesellschafter 136
Besetzung von Aufsichtsratsposten 544
Bestätigungsvermerk **361**
~, eingeschränkter **361**
Besteuerung öffentlicher Unternehmen (Betriebe) **288**
Betätigung der Gemeinde, wirtschaftliche 514
~ der öffentlichen Hand, wirtschaftliche 63
Beteiligung der Belegschaft **540**
~ der öffentlichen Hand an einem Unternehmen **101**
Beteiligungsbericht (der Bundesregierung) **103**
Beteiligungsrechte des Betriebsrats **551**

Beteiligungsunternehmen **99**
Beteiligungsverwaltung **104**, 350
Betrieb 116, 432
~, verstaatlichter 8
~ gewerblicher Art **58**
~, kommunaler **515**
~, kommunalisierter 8
~ öffentlicher 67, 68, 78, 80, 85
Betriebe und Unternehmen, öffentliche 59
Betriebsabrechnung 379, **401**
Betriebsauflagen **46**
Betriebsergebnis 379, **399**
Betriebsform **64**
Betriebsführung 40
~, marktwirtschaftliche **57**
Betriebsführungsgesellschaft 116
Betriebsführungsvertrag 116, **432**
Betriebsgesellschaft 116
Betriebskameralistik **378**
Betriebskosten 266
Betriebsleiter (eines Regiebetriebs) **119**, 120
Betriebsleitung **127**
Betriebsmittel **226**
Betriebsrat 537, **549**, 550
Betriebssatzung **121**
Betriebsvereinbarung 537
Betriebsvermögen **228**, 259
Betriebsverpachtung **229**
Betriebsversammlung 548
Betriebsvertrag, anzustrebender **303**
Bewertung 370
Bewertungsgrundsätze **370**
Beziehungen des Staates zum Staatsbürger 72
Bezirke der Fachaufsichtsbehörden für ge-

werblichen Straßenverkehr 507
Bezugsvertrag **534**
Bilanz **409**
Bilanzgewinn **410**
Bilanzstichtag **411**
Bilanzverlust **412**
Bildungswesen 2
Branntweinmonopol 85
Britische Bahnen 213
Bruttoveranschlagung 257
Buchführung 349, 357, **375**
~, doppelte kaufmännische **380**
~, erweiterte kameralistische **377**
~, gehobene kameralistische **379**
~, kameralistische **376**
~, ordnungsgemäße **375**
Buchwert **371**
Bund 31
Bundesbankgesetz 186
Bundeskartellamt **167**
Bürger 50
Bürgschaft, staatliche 214
Bürgschaften des Finanzministeriums 211
Bürgschaftsgewährung 211
Busunternehmen, kommunale 520

Cash Flow, diskontierter **306**

Dachgesellschaft 92
Darlehensaufnahme 218
Daseinsvorsorge **17**, 33
~ ohne Gewinnprinzip 3
Defizit **408**
Demarkationsvertrag **456**
Deputat **539**
Deutsche Bundesbahn 213
Deutsche Bundespost 213

Dienstvereinbarung **537**
Direktoren, geschäftsführende 135
~, nichthauptamtliche 135
Diskontierungssatz **304**
~, vorgeschriebener **305**
Doppik **380**
Dritter 116
Durchführungsorgane (der Regierung) 26
Durchschnittskosten 334, **340**

Effizienz öffentlicher Investitionsmittel 300
Effizienzstudien **316**
Eigenbetrieb(e) 85, 140, 433, **522**
Eigenbetriebe der Gemeinde 213
Eigenbetriebsgesetz **523**
Eigenbetriebsgesetze der Länder 523
Eigenbetriebsversorgung **523**
Eigenfinanzierung **224**
Eigengesellshaft **81**
Eigenkapital **262**, 409
Eigenkapitalausstattung einer öffentlichen Unternehmung **261**
Eigentum, öffentliches 41, 91
Eigentümer eines öffentlichen Betriebs 145
Eigenwirtschaft der öffentlichen Hand **1**
Eigenwirtschaftlichkeit **203**, 300
Einfluß, beherrschender **108**
Einheitstarif **502**
Einigungsstelle **555**
Einmanngesellschaft **90**, 91
Einnahmen und Ausgaben **405**

Einrichtung, öffentliche 83
~, parastaatliche gemeinnützige **166**
Einsatz von Steinkohle in Kraftwerken 482
Einstellung aus dem Jahresüberschuß in offene Rücklagen 424
~ von Personal **539**
Einwirkung der Aufsichtsbehörde **149**
Einzelbeanstandung **361**
Elektrizität 43, 452
Elektrizitätsnetz 472
Energieeinsparung **451**
Energiepolitik (für Brennstoffe) 448
Energieverbund **450**
Energieversorgungsunternehmen **452**
Energieverteilungsnetz **453**
Energiewirtschaft **449**
Energiewirtschaftsgesetz 194
Enquête, gesetzlich vorgeschriebene **165**
Enteignungsvollmacht 45, **157**
Entgelt **286**
~, privatrechtliches 282
Entlassung von Personal **539**
Entschädigung für Nationalisierung **181**
~ von Arbeitnehmern bei Beendigung des Arbeitsverhältnisses, gesetzlich vorgeschriebene 429
Entschließung, negative 196
~, positive 196
Entschuldung **254**
Entsorgung **487**
Entwässerung **487**
Entwicklung und Erschließung 13

123

Erdgas, flüssiges **478**
Erdgas-/Rohöl-Preise ab Bohrloch (Förderungsort) **480**
Erdölproduktion 449
Erfolgsplan **332**
Erfolgsrechnung **333**
Erhaltung des Vermögens **230**
Erlöse und Kosten **331**
Ermäßigungstarif **502**
Ermessenskontrolle **198**
Erneuerungsfonds **246**
Ersatzinvestition **231**
Erschließungsbeitrag **287**
Erstattungspflicht **267**
Erstattung für nichtkostendeckende Personenverkehrslinien **500**
Erstellung öffentlicher Leistungen **12**
Erster parlamentarischer Staatssekretär des Finanzministeriums 151
Ertrag 203
~ aus Erhebung gemeindlicher Grundsteuer auf Grundstückswerte 280
~ der Hebesätze 280
Erträge aus anderen Finanzanlagen **384**
~ aus Beteiligungen **383**
~ aus dem Abgang von Gegenständen des Anlagevermögens (Immobilien) **385**
~ aus der Auflösung von Rückstellungen **387**
~, betriebsbezogene **382**
~ und Aufwendungen **403**
Ertragslage 197
Ertragssteuern **293**
Ertragsziele **297**
~, vorgegebene **299**
Erweiterungsinvestition **231**

Erwerbswirtschaft **55**
erwerbswirtschaftlich **56**
Etatbindung des Regiebetriebs **257**
ERP-Sondervermögen 213
EVU **452,** 456

Fachaufsicht, ministerielle **155**
Fachaufsichtsbehörde **185, 506**
Fachbehörde, staatliche 155
Fachnormen für die Verwaltung öffentlicher Finanzen 353
Fahrpreise, ermäßigte ~ für Schüler 266
Fehlbetrag **408**
Fernheizung **455**
Fernverkehr **503**
Fernwärme 452, **455**
Feststellung des Betriebsergebnisses **400**
~ des Jahresabschlusses **392**
~ des Wirtschaftsplans **547**
Finanzanlagen **233**
Finanzautonomie **71**
Finanzbeziehungen zur Trägerkörperschaft **258**
Finanzierungsgesellschaft 221
Finanzinstitute der öffentlichen Hand **206**
Finanzmonopol **84**
Finanzplan **327**
Finanzplanung **325**
Finanzwesen 349
Fiskus **27**
Flughafenbehörde, britische 186, 204
Flugsicherungsanstalt 508
Förderung, direkte 269
~, indirekte 269

~ öffentliche **269**
Freiverband 113
Fremdkapital **264**
Funktionen öffentlicher Unternehmen 13

Gas 20, 43, 287, 452
Gebietskörperschaft(en) 2, 15, **31,** 40, 83
Gebote 50
Gebrauchserlaubnis **40**
Gebühr(en) 79, 277, **281,** 285
Gebührenanstalt **79, 285**
Gegenleistung, öffentlich-rechtliche 281
~, privatrechtliche 286
Geldmarkt **217**
Geldwert, in ~ gemessene Leistung **315**
Gemeindebetrieb 8
Gemeindeeigentum 37
Gemeindehaushalt **519**
Gemeinden 31, 488, 522
Gemeindeordnung **175**
Gemeinderat **516**
Gemeindeverbände 31
Gemeindevertreter im Werksausschuß **141**
Gemeineigentum **9**
gemeinnützig **4**
Gemeinnützigkeit **10**
Gemeinnützigkeitszwecke **265**
Gemeinwesen **11,** 81
Gemeinwirtschaft **3**
gemeinwirtschaftlich **4,** 56
Gemeinwirtschaftlichkeit **5**
Gemeinwirtschaftlichkeitswertung **6**
Gemeinwohl **7**
Gemeinwirtschaftsunternehmung **97**
Genehmigung einer Sondernutzung **42**
~, ministerielle **199**

124

∼ von Investitionsprogrammen 317
Genehmigungsvorbehalt 200
Genossenschaften 3
Gerichte 536
Gesamtheit der Rechtssätze 72a
Gesamtleistung 35
Geschäfte, zustimmungsbedürftige 201
Geschäftsbericht 357, 393
Geschäftsergebnis 298
Geschäftsführer 129
Geschäftsführung 128
Geschäftsjahr 390
Geschäftsleiter 130
Geschäftsleitung 127, 130, 349
Geschäftsordnung 125, 126
∼ erlassen, eine 125
Gesellschaft (AG, GmbH) 91
∼ mit beschränkter Haftung 95
Gesellschaftsrecht 87
Gesetze mit allgemeiner Gültigkeit 158
∼, parlamentarische 196
∼ zur Erteilung von Vollmachten an öffentliche Unternehmen 158
Gesetzentwurf 158
Gesetzesvorlagen 196
Gesetzgebung, untergeordnete 196
Gesundheitswesen 2
Gewährsträger 216
Gewerbetarif 473
Gewerkschaften 3, 535, 536
Gewinn 295, 417
∼, ablieferungsfähiger 293, 423
∼ erzielen 417
Gewinnablieferung 422

Gewinnbeteiligung 539
Gewinnermittlung, steuerliche 289
Gewinnerzielungsabsicht 54
Gewinnsteuern 293
Gewinn- und Verlustrechnung 418
∼ -/Verlustvortrag aus dem Vorjahr 419
Gezeitenenergie 462
Gezeitenstauwerk 463
GmbH(s) 91, 186, 357
Grafschaften 31
Grenzkosten 341, 334
∼, langfristige 341
Grund und Boden, öffentlicher 37
∼ und Boden, privater 37
Grundkapital 260
Grundlast 466
Grundsätze, betriebswirtschaftliche 96
Gründungsdatum eines Unternehmens 187
Gründungstag 187

Haftungsbeschränkung 88
Hand, öffentliche 16, 75, 98, 107, 108, 158
Handelsbilanz 396
Handelsrecht 86
Hauptsumme 222
Hauptversammlung 136
Haushalt des Trägers 118, 221
Haushaltsordnungen 211
Haushaltsplan der Gebietskörperschaft 433
∼ der Trägerkörperschaft 257
Haushaltssatzung 518
∼ vom Staat 519
Haushaltstarif 473
Heimfallrecht 44
Herstellungskosten 328

Hilfsbetriebe der Verwaltung 32
Hochspannungsleitung 465
Hoheitsbetrieb 69
Hoheitsträger 72
Hoheitsverwaltung 33, 50
Holding 92
∼ -Gesellschaft, öffentlich-rechtliche 93
∼ -Gesellschaft, staatliche 93
Individualverkehr 498
Inflationsbuchführung 372
Innenfinanzierung 223
Innenrevision 349
Inspektion 483
Institut für öffentliches Finanz- und Rechnungswesen, staatlich registriertes 353
Instrumentalunternehmen 25
Intendant 174
Interesse, öffentliches 7, 33
Internrevision 349
Investition 231
Investitionskreditfonds 525
Investitionsprogramme 317, 319
Investitionsrechnung 402
Investitionszuschuß 270

Jahresabschluß 392
∼ einer Aktiengesellschaft 357
Jahresbericht 393
Jahresbilanz 395
Jahreserfolgsrechnung 389
Jahresfehlbetrag 412
Jahresgewinn 410
Jahresplan, betrieblicher 322
Jahresüberschuß 416

Jahresverlust 412

Kameralistik 376
Kanalisation 488
Kanalisationsanlagen für Abwässer 485
Kapazitätsauslastung der Anlagen 470
Kapital 81
Kapitalausstattung 182, 239
Kapitalbedarf 238
Kapitalbeschaffung 240
~ auf dem Kapitalmarkt 240
Kapitalbeteiligung, staatliche 102
Kapitaldienst 241
Kapitalerhöhung 238
Kapitalerstausstattung 183
Kapitalgesellschaft 81, 95, 98
Kapitalhauptsumme 222
Kapitalherabsetzung 238
Kapitalmarkt 210, 217
Kapitalrationierung 313
Kapitalstock 239
Kapitalzuführung 239
Kapitalzuschuß 270
Kassenkredite der Bundesbank 212
Kernenergieentsorgung 487
Kernkraftwerk 461
Kilometertarif 502
Kinderheime 533
Kläranlage 487
Klärwerk 487
Kohlebergbau 449
Kohlepfennig 482
Kombinaton von Wettbewerb und Wohlfahrtsstaat 176
Kommunalaufsicht 517
Kommunalisierung 8
Kompetenz zum Erlaß spezifischer Richtlinien 194

Königliche Spezialagentur 170
~ Waffenfabrik(en) 172, 512
Konsortium 524
Kontokredit 189
Kontrahierungszwang 47
Kontrolle 155, 344
~, begleitende 347
~, externe 350
~, interne 349
~, parlamentarische 162, 348
~ über die Werkleitung ausüben 140
Konzept der allgemeinen ministeriellen Richtlinienkompetenz 192
Konzern 94
Konzernmuttergesellschaft 92
Konzernspitze 92
Konzession 38
~, eine ~ entziehen 38
~, eine ~ für eine Leistung erteilen 38
Konzessionsabgabe 39
Konzessionsbetrieb 38
Konzessionsgeber 38
Konzessionsnehmer 38, 46
Konzessionsträger 37
~ in der öffentlichen Versorgungswirtschaft 204
Konzessionsvertrag 37
Körperschaft, bundesunmittelbare 77
~ des öffentlichen Rechts 75
~, landesunmittelbare 76
~, nichtwirtschaftliche 83
~, öffentlich-rechtliche 111
~, staatliche 110
Körperschaften der öffentlichen Hand, wirtschaftliche 2

~ für neue Siedlungen 528
~, nichtministerielle öffentliche 74
Körperschaftssteuer 293, 294
Korrektur von Investitionsprogrammen 319
Kosten der Umweltverschmutzung 178
Kosten-Nutzen-Analyse 308
Kostendeckung 337
Kostendeckungsgrad 337
Kostendeckungsprinzip 337
Kostenechtheit der Preise (öffentlicher Leistungen) 337
Kostenmiete 273
Kostenrechnung 404
Kostensteuern 295
Kostenwirksamkeitsanalyse 309
Kraft-Wärmekopplung 454
Kraftwerk(e) 48, 461
Kredit- und Versicherungswesen, öffentliches 205
Kreditagenturen, kommunale 525
Kreditaufnahme 220, 312
~ beim Finanzministerium 210
~ bei nichtstaatlichen Stellen 211
~, öffentliche 237
Kreditbeschaffungspreise, indossierte 311
Kredite, staatliche 210
Kreditfonds des Finanzministeriums bei der Zentralbank 212
Kreditgewährung seitens der öffentlichen Hand 210
Kreditinstitut, öffentlich-rechtliches 207

126

Kreditplafond 160
Kreise 31
Kriterien für die Berufung von Vorstandsmitgliedern 186

Länder 31
Landkreise 31
Lasten, betriebsfremde 268
Lastenausgleichsfonds 213
Leistung, außertarifliche 539
~, hoheitlich geregelte öffentliche 51
~, öffentliche 282, 286
~, übertarifliche 539
Leistungsaufgaben 112
Leistungsfähigkeit des Betriebs 62
~, technische 62
~, wirtschaftliche 62
Leistungskriterium 197
Leistungstarif 502
Leistungsüberwachung 34
Leistungsverwaltung 33, 50
Leiter von Rundfunkanstalten 174
Leitungsmonopol, gesetzliches 43
Liegenschafts- und Mobilienverwaltung 78
Löhne und Gehälter 329
Löschung der Kapitalerstausstattungskredite 253
Luftfahrtkörperschaftsgesetz, britisches 188, 193

Marktwirtschaft, soziale 176
Mehrheits- und Minderheitsaktienbesitz 105

Mindestertrag, ministeriell vorgeschriebener 300
Minister, aufsichtsführender 150
Ministerien 311
Mitbestimmung 551
~, betriebliche 541
~ im Unternehmen 542
~, paritätische 543
Mitbestimmungsgesetz von 1976 542
Mitbestimmungsrecht 545
Mitbestimmung, überbetriebliche 544
Mittel, liquide 226
Mittelbeschaffung 219
Mittelverwendung 219, 326
Mitwirkung 551
~ der Behörden 75
Mitwirkungsrecht 546
Modell 13
Monopolverwaltung 85
Montanmitbestimmung 542
Morrisonsches Prinzip 110
Müllabfuhr 487, 488, 533
Müllverbrennung 487
Müllverbrennunganlage 487
Mustergeschäftsordnung 126
Mustersatzung 124

Nachkontrolle 346
Nachlaßverwalter 214
Nahverkehr 503
Nationale Girozentrale 215
Nationaler Kulturhistorischer Fonds 213
Nationales Kreditgesetz 210, 212
Nebenabreden 107
Nettoetatisierung 433

Nettogegenwartswert 307
Nettovermögenswert 197
Neuerung, technische 13
Neuinvestitionen aus beibehaltenen Gewinnen 224
nichtrechtsfähig 65
Niederspannungsleitung 465
Normen, geschäftliche 202
Nutzungserlaubnis 40
Nutzungsrecht an einer öffentlichen Sache 204
Nutzungsüberlassung 40
Nutzungsverleihung 40
Nutzwagenkilometer 504

Objektförderung 274
Opportunitätskosten 177
~, soziale 178
Organ, geschäftsführendes 132
Organisation des Staates 72
Organisationen, quasi-autonome nichtbehördliche 74

Parlament, dem ~ unterbreiten 196
Parlamentarischer Ausschuß für öffentliche Rechnungslegung 154
Pauschaltarif für Stromabgabe an Elektrizitätsversorgungsunternehmen 476
Pensionsfonds 214, 525
Pensionsrückstellungen 428
Person des öffentlichen Rechts, juristische 15, 66
~ des privaten Rechts, juristische 15, 66
~, juristische 66

127

Personal- und Sozialfragen 538
Personalrat 550
Personalverkehr, öffentlicher 494
Personalversammlung 548
Personalvertretung 550
Personen des Privatrechts 115
~ - und Sachgesamtheit 74
Personenbeförderungsfall 495
Personenkilometer 504
Personenverkehr auf der Schiene, unrentabler örtlicher 266
Personenverkehrsbehörde 496
Personenverkehrsbetrieb in Großstädten 497
Pflicht öffentlicher Monopolbetriebe 47
Pflichtprüfung 359
Pflichtverband 114
Planung 530
Planungsspielraum 323
Politik der Preisstabilisierung 180
~ des öffentlichen Auftragswesens (Vergabewesens) 438
Poolabkommen 338
(Präsident des) Rechnungshof(s) 355
Preisdämpfungsfunktion 335
Preispolitik für öffentliche Unternehmen 334
Preisregulierung 13
Primärenergie 446
Primärenergieversorgung 447
Prioritätsansetzung bei Investitionsvorhaben 314

Privatinitiative 63
Privatisierung 59
~ von *British Telecom* 489
~ der *British Gas Corporation* 489a
Privatwirtschaft 52
Produktivitätssituation 197
Proportion zwischen Eigen- und Fremdkapital 312
Prüfung 352
Prüfungsbericht (des Wirtschaftsprüfers) 360
Prüfungsergebnis 363
Prüfungsinstanz für die kommunale Verwaltung 356
Prüfungspflicht 358
Prüfungsverband 368
Prüfungsvermerk 361

Querverbund (von kommunalen Unternehmen) 520

Rationalisierungsinvestition 231
Rechenschaftslegung 36
Rechnungsabgrenzungsposten 430
Rechnungshof 350, **354**, **355**
Rechnungsprüfer 202
~, amtlich bestellter 364
Rechnungsprüfung 362
Rechnungsprüfungskollegium 369
Rechnungswesen 202, **374**
~, kaufmännisches 374
~, kommunales 519
~, öffentliches 374
Recht, öffentliches **72**, 72a
~ zur Kreditaufnahme 189

Rechte und Pflichten **188**
~ und Pflichten, arbeitsrechtliche 536
Rechtmäßigkeit einer übertragenen Aufgabe 155
Rechtsaufsicht 75, **345**
Rechtsbeziehungen 80
Rechtssetzungsbefugnis 123
rechtsfähig **65,** 74
Rechtsform **64**
Rechtsmäßigkeitskontrolle 345
Rechtspersönlichkeit **65**
Rechtsverordnung **195**, **196**
Regiebetrieb **118,** 257, 532, 379, 433
~, reiner 118
~, verselbständigter 522
Regiebetriebe, kommunale 213
Regionen 31
Reinertrag 197
Reserven, stille 424
Restbuchwert, nutzungsgerecht abgeschriebener 249
Rettungsaktion, wirtschaftliche 179
Rettung von Großkonzernen 178
Revision, interne 349
Richtlinienkompetenz **14,** 193
Rohaufwand 381
Rohertrag 381
Rücklage 424
~, eine ~ auflösen 424
~, eine ~ bilden 424
~, einer ~ Mittel entnehmen 424
Rücklagenentnahme 424
Rücklagekapital 424
Rücklagen, freie 426
~, gesetzliche 426
~, offene 426

Rückstellung(en) **246, 425**
~ für Abfindungen für Betriebszugehörigkeit **429**
~ für Geldentwertung **248**
Rundfunkanstalt **168**

Sachanlagen **234**
Sandilands-Bericht zur Inflationsbuchführung **372**
Satzung **121**
Satzungsgewalt **123**
Satzungsrecht **122**
Scheingewinn **421**
Schiedsgerichtsbarkeit **557**
Schlichtung **556**
Schottische Entwicklungsagentur **213**
Schuldendienst **241**
Schuldendienstleistung **251**
Seitenfinanzierung **221**
Sektor der Wirtschaft, privater **53**
~, öffentlicher **2**
Sekundärenergie **446**
Sekundärenergieversorgung **447**
Selbständigkeit, finanzielle **71**
Selbsteintritt 149
Selbsteintrittsrecht **149**
Selbstfinanzierung **224**
Selbstverwaltung **70,** 75
Selbstverwaltungskörperschaften 123
Selbstverwaltungsprinzip einer öffentlich-rechtlichen Körperschaft **111**
Sitzkapazitätenauslastung **505**
Sitzkilometer **504**
Sonderabmachungen **339**
Sonderabnehmer **474,** 475

Sonderabschreibung(en) **245, 255**
Sonderausschüsse des Parlaments **161**
Sonderbehörde **112a**
Sonderleistung, betriebliche **539**
Sondernutzung **41**
Sonderrechnung **432**
Sondertarif **473**
Sondervermögen **213**
Sondervertragskunden **475**
Sozialisierung **8,** 59
Sozialtarife **284**
Sozialversicherungsbeitrag **287**
Sparkassen **208**
Speicherkraftwerk **461**
Sperrminorität **106**
Spitzenbelastung, gleichzeitige **472**
Spitzenlast **466**
Spitzenlastdauerkurve **469**
Spitzentarifierung 334
Spitzenzeiten **467**
Staatsbeteiligungen **101**
Staatsbürger 72
Staatsmonopol **84**
Stabilitätspolitik **180**
Stadtkreise 31
Stadtwerke **8, 521**
Stammkapital **260,** 357
Standardisierung von Zinssätzen **310**
Stellenübersicht **554**
Steuerbefreiung **290**
Steuerbegünstigung **292**
Steuerbegünstigung für gemeinnützige Zwecke **265a**
Steuerbilanz **397**
Steuerermäßigung **292**
Steuern 277
Steuerprivileg öffentlicher Unternehmen **291**

Steuerung 13
Steuerungsausschuß **144**
Steuerverwaltung 27
Stiftung **82**
Straßenreinigung **487,** 488
Streitigkeiten 555
Strom 20
Stromerzeugungsanstalt, zentrale **457**
Stromerzeugungsmonopol öffentliches 457
Stromversorgungsnetz für das gesamte Staatsgebiet **460**
Stromverteilungsanstalten 458
~, regionale **459**
Subjektförderung **274**
Subsidiaritätsprinzip **63**
Substanzerhaltung **247**
Subvention für laufende Betriebskosten **270**
Subventionierung, finanzielle **276**

Tarif **282**
~, gespaltener 334, **475**
Tarifabnehmer **474**
Tarifgestaltung **283**
Tarifkunden 475
Tarifvertrag **536**
Tätigwerden, hoheitliches 72a
Teilkostendeckung **337**
Teilstreckentarif **502**
Telekommunikationssektor 489
Tilgung 241
Tilgungsanteil, progressiver 251
Tilgungsplan **250**
Träger **145, 524**
Träger öffentlicher Verwaltung 74
Trägerkörperschaft **145**
Trägerschaft **145**
Trägerverband **146, 524**
TÜV 115

Überbewertung **370**
Übernahme eines Unternehmens durch das Management **256**
Überprüfung, gerichtliche **163**
~, verwaltungsmäßige **164**
~ von Investitionsprogrammen **318**
Überschuß **415**
Überwachung der Geschäftsleitung **139**
Umlage **279**
Umlaufvermögen **227**
Umsatz **406**
Umsatzerlöse **407**
Umwandlung **89**
Unterbewertung **370**
Unterkonzern **94**
Unternehmen 10, 99, 137, 349
~, beherrschtes **109**
~ der öffentlichen Hand, privatrechtliche **95**
~, gemischtwirtschaftliches **98**, 108
~, kommunale 520
~ mit Mitbestimmung 538
~, nichtrechtsfähiges wirtschaftliches 522
~, öffentlich gebundenes **117**
~, öffentlich-rechtliche(s) **73**, 132
~, öffentliche(s) 14, **15**, 92, 158, 311
~, private gewerbliche 525
~, privatrechtliches 91
~, verbundenes **100**
Unternehmensform **64**
Unternehmensleitung **134**
Unternehmensplanung, mehrjährige **321**
Unternehmensrisiko **324**
Unternehmer, beliehene **115**

Unternehmerrisiko 116
Unternehmung, öffentliche 355
VDEW **458**
Veränderung des Lagerbestands **231**
Veräußerung von Vermögenswerten **236**
Verband Deutscher Elektrizitätswerke **458**
Verbindlichkeiten **24**, 264, 409
~ der kommunalen Sparkasse 216
Verbote 50
Verbraucherbeirat **169**
Verbund **48**
Verbundtarif **502**
Verbundvertrag **49**
Verbundwirtschaft **48**
Verdingungsordnung für Bauleistungen **442**
Verdingungsordnung für Leistungen, ausgenommen Bauleistungen **441**
Verfassungsrecht 72a
Verfügung, ministerielle **156**
Vergabe **439**
~, freihändige **445**
~ von Lieferungen **439**
~ von öffentlichen Aufträgen **439**
~ von öffentlichen Bauleistungen **439**
Vergabeart **440**
Vergabewesen **437, 438**
Vergesellschaftung **8**
Verglasung von Atommüll **484**
Verhandlungen, interministerielle 553
Verkehr, öffentlicher **491**
Verkehrs- und Versorgungsleistungen, kommunale 521

Verkehrsbetriebe **492**
Verkehrsgesetz (britisches) 194
Verkehrsleistungen 20
Verkehrstarife **502**
Verkehrsunternehmen 48, **492**
~ (im Eigentum) der öffentlichen Hand **493**
Verkehrsverbund **501**
Verkehrswegeerhaltung **511**
Verkehrswirtschaft **490**
Verlustabschreibung **252**
~ auf öffentliches Eigenkapital **255**
Verluste aus dem Abgang von Gegenständen des Anlagevermögens **386**
Verlustzuschuß **270**
Vermögen der Trägerkörperschaft 259
~, öffentliches 78
Vermögensgüter 246
Vermögenshaushalt 519
Vermögensplan **327**
Vermögensverwaltung 27, **28**
Vermögenswerte 40, 409
Verpachtung des Betriebsvermögens 229
Verpflichtung, finanzielle 197
~, soziale **18**
~ von nationalisierten Unternehmen, soziale **18**
Verpflichtungen des öffentlichen Dienstes **19**
Verselbständigung **67**
~, rechtliche **67**
~, wirtschaftliche **67**, **68**
Versicherungen 214
Versorgung **20**
Versorgungs- und Verkehrswirtschaft 48

Versorgungsauftrag **21**
Versorgungsbetrieb, gemeindlicher **534**
Versorgungsbetriebe der öffentlichen Hand **2**
Versorgungsgebiet **23**
Versorgungsgebiete von EVU **456**
Versorgungsnetz **23**
Versorgungsniveau **266**
Versorgungsunternehmen **534**
Versorgungswirtschaft **22, 490**
Verstaatlichung **8,** 59, 178
Verstromung **464**
Vertragsangebot **47**
Verwaltung 118, 379
~, ausgegliederte **436**
~, hoheitliche **50**
~ obrigkeitliche **50**
~, öffentliche 33, **72a**, **432**
Verwaltungsbetrieb 118
Verwaltungsdruckerei **69**
Verwaltungseinrichtung **83**
Verwaltungshaushalt **519**
Verwaltungsrat 132, 139, **143**, 392
Verwaltungsrecht **72a**
Verzinsung **241**
~ des Eigenkapitals, marktübliche **263, 301**
VOB **442**
VOL **441**
Vollbeschäftigungspolitik **180**
Vollkostenprinzip **343**
Vollmacht für Minister zur Erteilung von Anweisungen **191**
~ zur Aufnahme von Krediten **189**
~ zur Herausgabe allgemeiner Anweisungen **193**
~ zur Informationseinholung **190**

Vollmachten, gesetzlich auf dem Verordnungswege festgelegte **159**
Vorkontrolle **345**
Vorlage des Jahresberichts und Rechnungslegung **394**
Vorratsinvestition **231**
Vorstand **132,** 134, 135
~ in öffentlich-rechtlichen Unternehmen **143**
Vorstandsmitglied 137, 138
~, geschäftsführendes **137**
~, nichthauptamtliches **138**
Vortragen des Jahresgewinns auf neue Rechnung **420**
~ des Jahresverlusts auf neue Rechnung **414**

Wahl der Betriebsform aus steuerlichen Gründen **64**
Wärmekraftwerk **461**
Wasser 20, 287
Wasserkraftwerk **461**
Wasserleitung **488**
Wasserverbund **486**
Wasserversorgungs- und Abwasseranstalten **485**
Wegekosten **510**
Wegekostenrechnung **509**
Wegerecht **45**
Weisung 149
Weisungsgebundenheit **120**
Weisungsrecht **149**
Werkausschuß (des Eigenbetriebs) **140**
Werkleiter **130**
Werkleitung **130**
Wertberichtigungen **373**

Werterhöhung **235**
Wertminderung **235**
Wertpapiere, mündelsichere **214**
Wettbewerb 13
Wirtschaft, kommunale **514**
~, öffentliche **1**
wirtschaften **60**
wirtschaftlich betätigen, sich **60**
Wirtschaftsjahr **390**
Wirtschaftsbetriebe der öffentlichen Hand **358**
Wirtschaftsförderung **30**
~, regionale **30**
~, sektorale **30**
Wirtschaftsförderungsgesellschaft **29**
Wirtschaftsform 176
Wirtschaftsperiode **391**
Wirtschaftsplan **320**
Wirtschaftsprüfer **350, 365**
Wirtschaftsprüfungsgesellschaft(en) 357, **367**
Wirtschaftsprüfungswesen **366**
Wirtschaftstätigkeit, eine ~ ausüben **60**
Wirtschaftsunternehmen der öffentlichen Hand **3**
Wohngeld **274**
Wohnungsabteilungen, städtische **528**
Wohnungsbau, freifinanzierter **271**
~, öffentlich geförderter **272**
~, steuerbegünstigter **296**
Wohnungsbaugesellschaft, städtische **527**
Wohnungsbesitz, städtischer **526**
Wohnungsunternehmen, gemeinnütziges **528**

Wohnungsvereine, eingetragene 528
Wohnungswirtschaft 529
~, gemeinnützige 529

Zechenstillegung von unwirtschaftlichen Betrieben 481
Zeitwert 249
Zielsetzung, gemeinwirtschaftliche 4
Zielvorgabe 192
Zinsanteil, degressiver 251
Zins(satz), interner 302

Zivilluftfahrtsgesetz (britisches) 203, 204
Zonentarif 502
Zündwarenmonopol 85
Zusammenschluß von Gemeinden oder Gemeindeverbänden, rechtsfähiger 112
~ von kommunalen Verwaltungseinheiten 112
Zuschlag 342
Zuschläge auf Gewerbesteuer, gemeindliche 280
Zuschuß 270
~ zur Deckung von Betriebsverlusten 270
~ zur Deckung von Sonderlasten 270
Zuschüsse 500
Zuweisungen 246
Zwecke, gemeinnützige 265
Zweckmäßigkeit einer übertragenen Aufgabe 155
Zweckmäßigkeitskontrolle 351
Zweckverband 112, 524
Zweckverbände, regionale 485
Zwischenabschluß 398

Alphabetical Index

(The numbers following the words in the index refer to the numerically arranged list of words.)

AGM **136**
AGR 461
accountability of public sector **36**
~, social **5**
accountancy **366**
~ conventions 379
~ firm **367**
accounting **374**
~ deficit **412**
~ profit **410**
~, public sector **374**
accounts **202**
~, annual **392**
~ of a public limited company, annual 357
~ separate **432**
actions, administrative ~ by the State authorities 50
activities, economic ~ of a local authority 514
activity, economic ~ of public authorities 63
~, sovereign **72a**
Acts of Parliament 196
adjustment to investment programmes **319**
adjustments to valuations **373**
administration 118
~ of a monopoly **85**
~ of public services **33**
~ of State equity holdings **104**
~ of the assets of an undertaking **28**
~, public 33, 72a, 379
advancement of the public interest 265
advances, to obtain ~ from the Treasury 210

agencies, executive ~ of government **26**
agency, public 40, 116
agreement at the level of the enterprise **537**
~, collective **536**
agreements, collective ~ on wages and conditions 536
~, subsidiary **107**
Agricultural Marketing Boards **513**
Air Corporations Act 188, 193
Air Traffic Control Service **508**
Airport Authorities Act 186
alternatives, foregone 177, 178
amortization 241, 379
~ of public sector assets **243**
~ schedule **250**
Annual General Meeting **136**
Annual Report **393**
annuity **251**
anti-inflation policy **180**
application of resources **219**
approval of a special use **42**
~ of investment programmes **317**
~ of the annual accounts **392**
~ of the corporate plan **547**
arbitration **557**
~ commission 555
area boards for electricity

distribution **459**
~ served **23**
arm's length principle **111**
articles of association **121**
asset renewal fund **246**
assets **232**, 409
~, financial **233**
~, fixed **232**
~, net 197
~ of the owning body 259
~, physical **234**
association, compulsory **114**
~ of bodies ultimately responsible for a public enterprise **146**
~, voluntary **113**
associations of municipalities 31
attainment of operating autonomy **68**
audit **344**, **352**
Audit Commission for Local Government **356**
Audit Commissions for Central and Local Government 350
audit, compulsory **359**
~, concurrent 347
~, external **350**
~, financial **362**
~, internal **349**
~ outcome **363**
~, parliamentary **348**
~, post-hoc ~ of activity **346**
~, social **6**
~ team **369**
auditing of the annual accounts **357**

133

auditor, commercial 357, **365**
~, (official) **364**
auditors 202
auditor's certificate **361**
~ certificate, qualified **361**
~ report **360**
authorities, local 311, 488, 522, 525
~, public **16,** 75, 81, 98, 107, 108, 158
authority, ad-hoc **112, 112a**
~, joint **112**
~, local ~ accounts 433, 519
~, local ~ administration 432
~, local ~ budget **519**
~, local ~ enterprise 8
authority, local ~ property 37
~, local ~ undertaking 534
~, local ~ transport and utility provisions 512
~, local ~ utility 520
~, public 114, **147,** 355
~, sovereign 72
~, statutory 281
~, superior **148**
~, supervisory **149**
~, territorial 15, **31,** 83
autonomy, corporate **67**
~, economic **67**
~, financial **71**
~, legal **67**
~, operational 75
average cost(s) 334, **340**
award of contract by private agreement **445**

BBC 168
BSI 115
balance accounts, to **203,** 300
~ sheet **396, 409**

~ sheet, annual **395**
~ sheet drawn up for taxation purposes **397**
bank incorporated under public law 207
banking and insurance, public **205**
~ and insurance, public sector **206**
barrage, estuarial **463**
base load **466**
beachhead price of gas **479**
benefit, public 33
Bill **158**
bills, private 158
~, public 158
blocking minority shareholding **106**
board, executive **132**
~, joint **112**
~, joint ~ of local authorities 524
bodies, regional 485
~, non-departmental public 74
body corporate **66**
~ corporate under private law **66**
~ corporate under public law **66**
~, non-commercial 83
~, non-departmental public **166**
~ ultimately responsible for a public enterprise **145**
~ which supervises management 143
book value **371**
bookkeeping **375**
~, double entry **380**
~, correct **375**
~ within the framework of State accounting conventions **376**
borrowing powers **189**
Borrowing Powers Act **160**

borrowings **220, 264**
brandy monopoly 85
break even, to **203,** 300
British Airports Authority 204
~ Rail 213
broadcasting authority **168**
budget, administrative 519
~ appropriation for a trading fund activity **257**
~ estimates, gross 257
~ of the owning authority 221, **257**
~ of the owning body 118
~ regulations 211, 518
budgeting on a net basis **433**
building societies incorporated under public law 209
bulk supplies for local distribution 534
~ supply tariff **476**
bus undertakings, municipal 520
business accounting **374**
~ established under private law, public sector **95**
~ horizon **391**
~ incorporated under private law 15
~ incorporated under public law 15
~, publicly-owned **15**
~, to carry on a **60**
~ unit, non-autonomous **69**
~ with mixed ownership **98**
~ year **390**
businesses established under public law 132
bye-laws **523**

CEGB **457**
CHP **454**
Co. Ltd. **91, 95**
cameralistics **376, 378**
capital 81
∼ account **402**
∼ allowance against tax **243**
∼ appreciation **238**
∼ assets 246, 248
∼ assets, movable 78
∼ budget 519
∼, circulating **227**
∼ debt **182**
∼ debt, commencing **183**
∼, external **264**
∼, fixed **232**
∼ fund **239**
∼ grant **270**
∼ market 210, **217**
∼ rationing **313**
∼ reconstruction **254**
∼ requirements **238**
∼ reserve **424**
∼ restructuring **255**
∼ servicing **241**
∼ working **226, 228,** 259
capitalization **239**
carrier obligation, common **499**
carrying forward a deficit **414**
∼ forward a profit **420**
cash advances extended by the Bundesbank 212
∼ balances **226**
∼ flow, discounted **306**
∼ limits on spending in nominal terms **311**
Central Electricity Generating Board **457**
certification (of completion of work) **531**
change of corporate form **89**
changes in fixed capital **232**

∼ in stocks **231**
charge, commercial **286**
∼, statutory 277, **287**
∼, statutory ∼ for usage **281**
charges 203
∼ agreed **339**
charging agreements **339**
Chartered Institute of Public Finance and Accountancy **353**
chief executive of a public body **173**
Chief Secretary to the Treasury **151**
children's homes 533
choice of legal form for tax reasons 64
citizen 50, 72
Civil Aviation Act 203, 204
coal mining 449
coal *Pfennig* 482
co-determination 551
∼ above the level of the firm 544
Co-determination Act of 1976 542
co-determination at the level of the firm 541
∼ – ∼, equal 543
∼ – ∼ in enterprises 542
combination of competition and welfare State 176
∼ of human and material resources 74
∼ of local authorities 112
combined heat and power **454**
comment, qualified **361**
committee, executive **132**
∼ for a nationalized industry, organizing **184**
∼ supervisory 132
committees of Parliament, select **161**

commonality **11**
community service function 50
companies, private 357
∼, public limited 132
company 99
∼ formed to raise capital 221
∼ forming part of an industrial group **100**
∼ incorporated under private law 91
∼, joint-stock 81, **95,** 98
∼, joint-stock ∼ wholly owned by the public sector **81**
∼, joint-stock ∼ with only one owner **90**
∼ law **87**
∼ pension scheme **552**
∼, public **91**
∼, public limited 89, **95,** 135, 136
∼, subsidiary **109**
∼ with limited liability **95**
compensation for nationalization of assets **181**
∼ for public service obligations **266**
competence, legislative 123
competition 13
complaints 149
Comptroller and Auditor General **355**
concept of general direction as given by Ministers **192**
concession **38**
∼ contract 37
∼ for the performance of a service, to grant a **38**
∼ giver **38**
∼, to withdraw a **38**
concessionaire **38,** 46
conditions of service 536, 537, **539**

135

~ of service, enhanced 539
conflicts 555
connection, compulsory 488
~ obligation, compulsory 47
consent of the Minister 199
~, qualified 200
Consolidated Fund 211
consortium 112, 524
construction of housing, free-market 271
~ or civil engineering enterprise 532
consumer 474
~ by negotiated price 474
Consumer Council 169
consumer on standard tariff 474
contract customers, special 475
~ of employment 536, 539
~ to secure (horizontal) integration 49
contractor 61
contracts procedure 440
contribution 279
~, compulsory 277, 287
~ paid for connecting a new development to public utility 287
control 133, 344
~, ministerial 155
~ of commanding heights of the economy 13
~, parliamentary 162
~, supervisory 155
~ to ensure that processes and measures confirm to objectives 351
~ to ensure that proposals conform to

regulations 345
~, to ~ the operational management 140
conversion to electricity 464
cooperatives 3
corporation established under public law 75
~, public 73, 75
~, statutory 75
~ tax 294
cost accounting 404
~ benefit analysis 308
~ effectiveness analysis 309
~, marginal 334
~ of pollution 178
~ pricing, full 343
cost-rent 273
costs, long-run marginal 341
~, marginal 341
council, municipal 516
counties 31
courts 536
credit-financed spending 311
~ granted by public authorities 210
criteria of appointing boards 186
Crown Agents 170
Crown Servants 172

DCF 306
DLO 118a, 532
date on which balance is struck 411
day, appointed ~ of an undertaking 187
debt servicing 241
~ servicing payment 251
decision-making body of shareholders 136
deficit 408, 412
~, annual 412
~ subsidy 270
delivery contract 534

demand, simultaneous maximum 472
demarcation 259
~ agreement 456
department, supervising 185
Departments of Technical Services 521
depreciation 243
~, anticipated 243
~ at historic cost 243
~ at replacement cost 243
~ through market obsolescense 243
~ through technical obsolescence 243
~, unanticipated 243
determination, ministerial 156
~ of taxable profits by the fiscal authorities 289
development agency, economic 29
~ and planning 13
direct labour organization 118a, 532
directive 149
Director-General 174
Director, Managing 129
~ of Personnel 538
directors, executive 134, 135
~, non-executive 135
discount rate 304
dismissal of personnel 539
district heating 452, 455
districts 31
~, metropolitan 31
dividend capital, public 261
division within a group 94
dominance, sectoral 13
drainage and sewage disposal 485
duty, financial 197

∼ to compensate, legal 267
∼ to comply with instructions 120

EFL **312**
earning situation 197
easement **45**
economy, mixed **97**
∼, private **52**
∼, profit-motivated **55**
∼, social market **176**
education services 2
efficiency measure for public investment 300
∼ studies **316**
electricity 20, 43, 452
Electricity Council **458**
electricity industry 458
∼ supply cable, high tension **465**
∼ supply cable, low tension **465**
∼ supply grid 472
elimination of uneconomic mining capacity **481**
employer 536
employers association 536
energy conservation **451**
∼ distribution network **453**
∼ industries **449**
∼, primary **446**
∼, secondary **446**
∼, tidal **462**
∼ supply undertaking **452**
enterprise 10, 137, 349, 432
∼, autonomous municipal 140
∼, commercial or industrial **58**
∼, concessionary **38**
∼ established under public law **73**
∼, local ∼ boards **525**

∼, municipal 8, 433, **514**
∼, public 14, 67, 68, 78, 80, 85
∼, publicly regulated **117**
∼ with mixed public/private sector participation 108
enterprises in public ownership, economic 2
∼, not-for-profit **3**
∼ of the State, public 311
∼, private-sector industrial 525
∼, public 3, 59, 92, 158
enterprises, public ∼ group in the Treasury **152**
∼ run by the public sector, commercial 358
∼ which have co-determination 538
entity, administrative **83**
Equalization of War Burdens Fund 213
equity capital **260,** 357
∼ shareholding: majority and minority **105**
European Recovery Program Special Fund 213
example, to set an 13
Exchequer advances **210**
Exchequer and Audit Department 354
Executive Board 392
∼ Board Member **137**
∼ Board of Management 135
exercise of government as a regulatory function **50**
expediency of delegated functions 155
expenditure 203
∼, gross **381**
∼ on capital account 519
∼ (on factor inputs) **388**
∼, public 153

∼ surveys, public **153**
extent to which costs are recovered **337**
∼ to which prices (of public services) reflect true costs **337**
External Financing Limits **312**
extinguishment of capital debt **253**

facility, public 41
fare structure, integrated **502**
fares for school children, reduced 266
Federal corporation 77
∼ Government 31
∼ institution 77
fee-charging institution **79, 285**
fees and charges 79, 285
finance, internal **223**
financing, lateral 221
firms of auditors 350
fiscal law **278**
fixed-interest securities 214
forecasting, financial **325**
form of an enterprise, legal **64**
foundation **82**
"fringe benefit", enhanced **539**
fuel industries, primary **447**
∼ industries, secondary **447**
∼ policy **448**
functions of a specific enterprise 40
∼ of the State, sovereign 33, **50**
fund, specially designated **213**

gas 20, 43, 287, 452
∼, liquid natural **478**

137

generating monopoly, public 457
German Energy Act 194
~ Federal Bank Act 186
~ Federal Post Office 213
~ Federal Railways 213
Government advances 210
~ bodies, central and local 2
~ body, joint local ~ ~ with legal status 112
~ intervention 75
~ regulations 518
grant to organizations providing housing with public subsidy 275
grants for unremunerative passenger services 500
grid, national 460
group, industrial 94
guarantees on loans 211
guarantor 216

head, administrative 129
~ of broadcasting organizations 174
health services 2
H.M. Inspectorates 483
holding company 92
~ company organized under public law 93
housing 529
~ association, registered 528
~ benefit paid to an individual 274
~ construction promoted by tax concessions 296
~ departments, municipal 528
~, public sector 529
~ stock, municipal 526
~ subsidized by public

funds 272
~ undertakings, municipal 527
~ undertakings, public 528
incineration of solid waste 487
income and expenditure 405
~ from cancellation of reserve provisions 387
~ from disposals of assets 385
~ from financial deposits 384
incorporation under company law 68
increase in capital 238, 239
~ in value 235
independence, financial 71
index-linking of prices in contracts 336
individuals organized under private law 115
inflation accounting 372
influence, dominating 108
influencing prices 13
initiative, own 149
~, private 63
Inland Revenue 27
innovation, technological 13
institute of chartered accountants 368
institution established under public law 74
~, public 74, 79, 83, 285
insurance companies 214
integration, horizontal 48
~ of energy systems 450
interest payments 241
~ payments, decreasing 251
~ payments (nominal) on owner's equity, at market rates 301

~ public 7
interim accounts 398
intervention of the supervisory authority 149
inventories 231
investment 231
~ agencies 525
~ in stocks 231
~ income 383
~ from retained profits, new 224
~ programmes 317, 319
~ review 318
~ subsidy 270
~ which increases capacity 231
~ which rationalizes production stocks 231
invitation to tender, public 443
~ to tender, restricted 444
~ to tender with public competition from an approved list, restricted 444

LNG 477, 478
LWR 461
Laender 31
land and property 78
Land corporation 76
Land institution 76
Land legislation 523
law, administrative 72a
~, commercial 86
~, constitutional 72a
~ of reversion 44
~, public 72, 72a
~, statutory 122
leasing of working capital 229
legality of delegated functions 155
legislation, secondary 196
letting out 439
level of performance tariff 502

levy **277,** 278
∼, concessionary **39**
liabilities **24, 264,** 409
∼, deferred **430**
liability of a municipal savings bank 216
limit to borrowing by public enterprises 312
limitation of liability **88**
line manager **130**
load duration curve **469**
∼ factor **468**
∼ -shedding **471**
loans raised from non-Government sources 211
Local Government Act **175**
loss, annual **412**
losses from disposals of assets **386**

(Main) Board of Directors **134**
maintaining the real value of capital assets **247**
maintenance of working capital **230**
making up the deficit of a municipal enterprise **413**
management **128,** 349
∼, autonomous **436**
∼ buy-out **256**
∼ committee, senior 144
management contract **116**
∼ contractor 116
∼ in enterprises established under public law 143
∼ of an enterprise **127,** 537
∼, operational **130**
manager, executive **131**
∼ (of a direct labour organization) **119**
∼ of a trading fund activity 120

manpower forecast **554**
market rate of return on equity **263**
matches monopoly 85
measures to maintain a high level of employment 180
mediation **556**
meeting of employees, general 548
∼ the cost of acquired liabilities **431**
Member of a Board of Directors 137, 138
member, elected ∼ of a local authority **141**
merit order system **314**
methods of depreciation **244**
Minister, the responsible ∼ (sponsoring) **150**
ministries 311
model articles of association **124**
∼ rules of procedure **126**
money market **217**
Monopolies and Mergers Commission **167**
monopoly, financial **84**
Morrisonian principles **110**
municipalities 31

NPV **307**
National Audit Office **354**
National Giro Bank **215**
National Heritage Fund 213
National Loans Act 210, 212
National Loans Fund **212**
nationalization **8**
negotiations, inter-departmental 153
new town corporations 528
nomination to seats on Supervisory Boards 544
Non-Executive Board Member **138**
normalization of interest rates **310**

OFGAS **489a**
OFTEL **489**
objectives, financial **297**
obligation on public monopoly enterprises 47
∼ to balance revenue accounts **203**
obligation to break even **203**
obligations **24**
∼, externally imposed **268**
∼, public service **19**
∼, social ∼ of nationalized industries **18**
Office of Telecommunications **489**
official, public **171**
oil production 449
operate, to ∼ commercially **57**
operating conditions **46**
∼ costs 266
∼ in the public interest without a profit motive **4,** 56
∼ in the pursuit of profit **56**
∼ obligations **46**
∼ plan, annual **322**
opportunity costs **177**
∼ costs, social **178**
order, ministerial **156**
∼, statutory 195
orders 50
organ, executive 132
organization of the State 72
organizations, quasi-autonomous non-

139

governmental 74
orientation to public service **10**
overdrafts 189
overvaluation **370**
owner **524**
∼ of a public enterprise 145
owners **524**
owner's equity **262,** 409
ownership, municipal 8
∼, public **9,** 91
∼, social **8**

PAC **154**
PLC **91, 95**
PSBR **237**
PTA **496**
PTE **497**
PWR 461
Parliament, to lay before 196
participation 551
∼ of the workforce **540**
party, third 116
passenger journey **495**
∼ kilometres **504**
∼ transport authority **496**
∼ transport executive **497**
∼ transport, local public **494**
payment made under private law 282
payments "above the going rate" **539**
peak load **466**
∼ -load tariff 334
∼ periods **467**
pension funds 525
performance, commercial **298**
∼ control **198**
∼ criterion **197**
∼, financial 349, 357
∼ monitoring **34**
∼ overall **35**

permission to use public resources **40**
personality, devoid of legal **65**
∼, having legal **65**
∼, legal **65,** 74
personnel and social questions 538
pit closures **481**
placing **439**
∼ of public construction work **439**
∼ of public contracts **439**
∼ of supply contracts **439**
plan, corporate **320**
∼, rolling corporate **321**
planning **530**
∼ margin **323**
plant loading **470**
policy-based agencies **25**
∼ -setting committee **140, 143**
pooling arrangement 338
power grids 48
∼ of compulsory purchase **157**
∼ of direction **14**
∼ of Ministers to issue directions to nationalized industries **191**
∼ of Ministers to require information **190**
∼ of specific direction **194**
∼ station **461**
∼ station, hydroelectric **461**
∼ station, nuclear **461**
∼ station, pumped storage **461**
∼ station, thermal **461**
∼ to issue general directions **193**
powers and duties **188**
∼ of compulsory purchase **45**
∼ of the Executive, judicial 72a
∼ of the Executive, quasi-judicial 72a
∼ to raise loans 189
precept **279**
presentation of annual report and accounts **394**
pricing policies of nationalized industries **334**
principle of capital replacement **242**
∼ of last resort **63**
∼ of recovering costs **337**
principles of operating in a commercial manner **96**
printing department within an administration 69
privatization **59**
∼ of British Telecom **489**
∼ of the British Gas Corporation 489a
procurement, public **438**
∼ system **437**
production costs **328**
productivity 197
profit **417**
∼ and cost account **403**
∼ and cost account for a specific cost centre **331**
∼ and loss account **333**
∼ and loss accounting **418**
∼ and loss forecast **332**
∼, annual **410**
∼, apparent **421**
∼, gross 295
∼ /loss carried forward from the previous year **419**
∼ motive **54**
∼ -sharing **539**
∼, to make a **417**
profits, net 293

∼ taxes **293**
∼ transferable **423**
prohibitions 50
promotion of economic development **30**
∼ of economic development, regional **30**
∼ of economic development, sectoral **30**
property agency **78**
∼ board **78**
∼, private 37
∼, public 37
provision for depreciation **246**
∼ for depreciation, special **245**
∼ for inflation **248**
∼ for pension payments **428**
∼ for pensions and social support payments **427**
∼ for statutory redundancy payments 429
∼ of public utilities **20**
∼, private sector ∼ of local authority services under contract **533**
∼, public **12**
Public Accounts Committee **154**
∼ Enquiries **165**
∼ Sector Borrowing Requirement **237**
purchasing policy, public **438**
purposes, charitable **265**
∼ for which public enterprises are established **13**

QUANGO(s) 74, 166

RRR **300**
railway passenger services, uneconomic local 266
raising a loan **218**
∼ capital **240**
∼ capital in the market **240**
∼ of external capital **225**
∼ of funds **219**
∼ of resources **219**
rate of return 197
∼ of return, internal **302**
∼ of return, required **300**
∼ poundage multiplied by rateable value – in local government finance 280
∼ product **280**
records, financial 349, 357
recovery of costs **337**
∼ of costs, partial **337**
recruitment of personnel **539**
reduction in capital **238**
∼ in value **235**
∼ schedule **250**
redundancy fund reserve **429**
∼ payments **553**
refuse collection 533
∼ disposal 488
Regional Water Authorities **485**
regions 31
Regulations **196**
∼ governing the affairs of local undertakings **523**
relation of owner's equity to external capital 312
relations, industrial **535**
∼ of the State with the citizen 72
relationship, legal **80**
relationships with the ultimate owning body, financial **258**
repayment of capital 251
replacement investment **231**
Report of the Federal Government on participant State equity holdings 103
representative of the work force in the policy committee **142**
requirement to be audited **358**
requirements, financial **238**
rescue of major companies 178
reserve fund **424**
∼ fund, to wind up a **424**
∼ provision **425**
∼, to build up a **424**
∼, to release a **424**
reserves, declared **426**
∼, free and untrammeled **426**
∼, legally required **426**
∼, statutorily required **426**
∼, to draw from **424**
∼, undeclared **424**
resolution, negative 196
resources 40
responsibility, practical social ∼ in an active sense **17**, 33
∼, social ∼ without profit 3
revenue 203
∼ from the primary activity of the enterprise **382**
∼ grant **270**
∼, gross **381**
∼ pooling (in municipal undertakings) 520
review, administrative **164**
∼, judicial **163**
right of co-determination 545
∼ of participation of the works council 546
∼ of the works council

141

to be involved 551
~ to action on own initative **149**
~ to issue bye-laws **123**
~ to issue directives **149**
~ to raise objection **149**
~ to use public property 204
rights and duties under labour law 536
~ of supervision **149**
risk, commercial 116
~, entrepreneurial **324**
Royal Ordnance Factories 172, **512**
rules of procedure 126

SGHWR 461
sales **406**
~ of assets **236**
~ receipts **407**
salvage operation, economic **178**
Sandilands Report on inflation accounting **372**
savings banks **208**
Scottish Development Agency 213
seat kilometres **504**
seating load factor **505**
sector of the economy, private **53**
~ of the economy, public **1**
~, public **2**
security, social ~ contribution(s) **287, 330**
self-administration **70**
~ -financing **224**
~ -governing bodies 123
~ -government **70**
separation **434**
~ for accounting purposes of a municipal enterprise from local authority administration **435**
servant, civil **171**

service 112
~, public **282**
~, public ~ employee 119
~, statutorily regulated public **51**
services of a public administration, auxiliary **32**
~, in-house **118**
setting objectives in the public interest 4
sewage 287
~ and refuse disposal services **487**
~ disposal **487**
~ works **487**
sewerage 488
share, golden **106**
shareholders funds **262**
shire districts 31
shortfall **408**
sinking fund **246**
society in a social sense **11**
stabilization policy 180
staff association 550
staff council 550
standard building contracts in the public sector **442**
~ fare **502**
~ of service 266
~ price 502
~ terms and conditions for the supply of goods and services to public bodies **441**
standards, commercial 202
~ of competence in public sector financial managements 353
standing orders **125**
~ orders, to promulgate **125**
State accounting system, expanded **377**
~ accounting system with capital entries included, single entry **379**
~ accounting conventions used in enterprises **378**
~ as financial body **27**
~ corporation 110
~ equity holding **102**
~ holding company **93**
~ monopoly **84**
~ -owned enterprise **8**
~ participation **101**

statement, financial ~ for the year **389**
~ of capital position **232**
Statutory Instrument **196**
~ Instruments Act 196
~ Powers and Instruments **159**
steering committee **144**
street cleansing **487,** 488
subsidy 270
~, direct **269**
~, indirect **269**
~ on dwelling construction **274**
~, public **269**
~ to cover the losses of an enterprise **270**
~ to meet special obligations **270**
sum, principal **222**
summary of operating accounts **401**
supervision **133**
~, legal 75
~ of local authority affairs **517**
~ of the management **139**
Supervisory Board **135,** 139, 392, 542
supplements to Local Business Tax, locally determined 280
supplies contracts, inter-

142

ruptible **477**
supply agreement 47
~ area **23**
~ areas for energy undertakings 456
~ monopoly, statutory **43**
~ network **23**
support, financial **276**
surcharge **342**
surplus **415**
~, annual **416**
~, transferable **423**
system, economic 176
systems audit **351**

taking into public ownership 178
~ into social ownership 59
~ into State ownership **8,** 59
~ note of trading results **400**
target rate of return **303**
~ setting 192
targets, financial **299**
tariff **282**
~, concessionary **284, 502**
~ customers 475
~, domestic **473**
~, industrial **473**
~, multi-part 334, **475**
~, negotiated **473**
~ per kilometre **502**
~, staged **502**
~ structure **283**
~, zoned **502**
tax concession 292
~ concessions for charitable purposes **265a**
~ exemption 290
~ privileges of public enterprises 291
~ reduction 292
taxation of public enterprises **288**

taxes 277
~ on costs 295
telecommunications sector 489
test discount rate **305**
time of vesting **187**
totality of the legal provisions 72a
track costs **510**
~ maintenance **511**
trade union enterprises 3
~ unions 535, 536
trading fund activities 379, 433
~ fund activity **118,** 257
~ fund activity devoid of legal personality, operationally autonomous 522
~ fund activity, municipal 89, 213
~ performance 379
~ result **399**
Traffic Areas **507**
~ Commissioners **506**
traffic, individual **498**
~, local **503**
~, long-distance **503**
transactions which require approval **201**
transfer of profits **422**
~ of surplus **422**
transferring trading surplus to resources **424**
Transport Act 194
transport cost calculation **509**
~, public 48, **491**
~ sector **490**
~ system, integrated **501**
~ tariffs **502**
~ undertakings 20, **492**
~ undertakings, public **493**
Treasury 27
treasury function (in an administration or enterprise) **28**

~ guarantees **211**
Trustee Investment Act 214
~ Investments **214**
trustees 214
turnover **406, 407**

UK Government Agency 170
undertaker, contracted **115**
~, statutory 37, **204**
undertaking, (local) autonomous **522**
~, municipal **515, 521**
~ owned by more than one organization **99**
undertakings, autonomous municipal 213
~, statutory ~ in public ownership 2
undervaluation **370**
usage, compulsory **488**
use of a public service 282, 286
~ of assets, projected **327**
~ of coal in power stations 482
~ of public facilities 281
~ of resources **326**
~ of resources in volume terms 311
~, special **41**
users, special 475
using public enterprises to hold down prices in a particular sector of the economy **335**
utilities, public **22, 490**
utility, public ~ and transport undertakings 48
~ service 21

VFM **315**
valuation **370**
~ principles **370**
value for money **315**

143

~, net present **307**
~, written-down ~ reflecting physical use **249**
vehicle kilometres **504**
vesting date **187**
viability, economic 62
~ of an enterprise **62**
~, technical 62
vitrification of nuclear waste **484**

wages and conditions agreement **536**
~ and salaries **329**
~ in kind **539**
waste, radioactive ~ disposal **487**
~, solid ~ incinerator **487**
~ water disposal **487**
wastes, solid ~ disposal **487**
water 20, 287
~ supply **488**
~ supply system, integrated **486**
wayleave **45**

well-head price of gas/oil **480**
withdrawal from reserves **424**
work force, municipal 532
works council 537, 549, 550
writing off **238**
~ off capital **252**
~ off capital debt **253**
~ off public dividend capital 255
year, financial **390**